'BORN FREE'

STUDIES IN GALATIANS

GEORGE MITCHELL

This book is dedicated to:

ANGUS

Our activist three-year-old Grandchild

About the Author

George Mitchell was born and raised in Glasgow, Scotland, and was converted and trained for Christian service at Lambhill Evangelical Church, and London Bible College (now London School of Theology).

George spent five years as a metallurgist in the steel industry, seventeen years as a full-time teacher and lecturer, and over twenty years as a Baptist pastor in Scotland. He is guest lecturer at the International Christian College, Glasgow ,and Scott Theological College, Machakos, Kenya.

George enjoys football, badminton, golf and trumpet-playing. George and Jean have been married since 1964, and have a married son, Finlay, a married daughter, Janet, and two grandchildren, Kirstin and Angus.

Goerge has had four books published – 'Comfy Glasgow', a personal testimony, 'Chained and Cheerful', a commentary on Philippians, 'Revival Man' the story of Jock Troup, revivalist-evangelist, and 'Prisoner for Christ', a biography of John Bunyan for young people.

This book arose from a series of broadcast talks given on Revival FM, a local Christian radio station in Cumbernauld, near Glasgow. This explains the conversational rather than academic style, hopefully, suitable for people of faith, and people of no faith. I have edited the scripts, and included chapter summaries and questions for discussion, which could be a help to Bible Study groups. I have included a 'Digging Deeper' section, which comments on some textual matters which will, hopefully, help people to understand and be inspired by this wonderful letter.

I am grateful to my colleagues at Revival FM, particularly Dorian Stone, for their help in the studio, and to the Board of Directors for permission granted to work on the scripts.

The book goes out with the hope that God will graciously bless this piece of work.

As always, I am debtor to many people, including the library ladies Gwenda, Gudrun and Lucy at the International Christian College, and to all the staff, especially Kenneth and Jim at Kenwil Print and Design, the printers, but most of all to Jean, my wife, pal, guide, counsellor, and general factota...

A WORD ABOUT THE TITLE.

'Born Free' is a good title for Galatians. The letter has a good and long pedigree in the story of the Church and the origins of the Reformation.

In 1513 (yes, as long ago as that!) , Martin Luther, the thirty-year old professor of Biblical Studies at Wittenberg University in Germany, began a series of lectures on The Psalms, and the New Testament letters Romans, Galatians and Hebrews. Haunted by his own sense of sinfulness : 'I, a miserable pigmy.... Dust and ashes and full of sin', Luther emerged from his studies with a new concept of God. Through the Cross of Christ the all-terrible God before whom Luther trembled, revealed Himself as the gracious God, his wrath meeting His mercy in the wonder of redeeming love. As for humanity, they should give up all reliance upon themselves, come to terms with their continuing unworthiness, and accept God's goodness with belief, trust and commitment. Luther saw that this was what the apostle Paul meant when he quoted the Old Testament prophet Habakkuk: 'The just shall live by faith'. This is the meaning of justification by faith, and this is what lay at the basis of Reformed thinking. This was like a new birth into a life of freedom.

The message of Galatians is as relevant today as when its light shone upon Martin Luther. It has been over eighty years since mainland Britain saw a Biblical Revival, and Christians are struggling to find their bearings. The world as an anti-God system exerts tremendous pressure on the Church and the Bible. The political systems have adopted a secular humanist philosophy which marginalises the Church and ridicules the Christians, despite the enormous contribution made by the Lord's people to lift up the helpless and minister to the casualties in the rat-race of modern life. Vast amounts of money are being spent, and huge efforts are being made to find peace through 'alternative religion'. This all confirms that we are worshipping beings made with a Godward reference.

Some of the influential Christian groups, particularly those involved in training for Christian service, have undermined confidence in the Bible, have swallowed post-modernist ideas, and promote 'user friendly' techniques and courses as answers to our spiritual problems.

In Galatians, the apostle Paul tells us, as God's accredited servant, that performance, ritual, and self-effort can never bring peace with God. Getting us fit to face God is not something we do, but something Christ has done for us, becoming a curse for us on the Cross to set us free. The way to be born free is to trust in God's grace alone, in Scripture alone, and in Christ's sacrifice alone, without additions or embellishments. I was therefore delighted to write about this wonderful letter, and pray that many may be 'born free' as a result of reading it....

SOURCES.

WF Arndt-FW Gingrich. A Greek-English Lexicon of the New Testament and Other Early Christian Literature. Cambridge University Press. 1957.

W Barclay. The Letters to the Galatians and Ephesians. Daily Study Bible or St Andrew Press, Edinburgh, 1959.

FF Bruce. Paul, Apostle of the Free Spirit. Paternoster Press. Carlisle, 1992.

RA Cole. The Epistle of Paul to the Galatians. Tyndale Press, London, 1969

JD Douglas, ed. The Illustrated Bible Dictionary. IVP/Tyndale Press.Leicester, 1988.

RKY Fung. The Epistle to the Galatians. New International Commentary or WB Eerdmans, Grand Rapids, Michigan, 1989.

GW Hansen. Galatians. IVP New Testament Commentary series. Leicester, England, 1994

C. R. Hume. Reading through Galatians. SCM Press, London, 1997.

AM Hunter. Galatians to Colossians. Layman's Bible Commentary. SCM Press, London, 1960.

GF Hawthorne, RP Martin, DG Reid, eds. Dictionary of Paul and His Letters. IVP, Leicester, England, 1993.

LA Jervis. New International Bible Commentary: Galatians. Hendrickson Publishers Inc. Peabody, Massachusetts., 1999.

S Kubo. A Reader's Greek-English Lexicon of the New Testament and a Beginner's Guide for the Translation of New Testament Greek. Zondervan Publishing House, Grand Rapids, Michigan, 1975.

M. Luther. Commentary on the Epistle to the Galatians. James Clarke, 1953.

S McKnight. Galatians. The NIV Application Bible. Zondervan, Grand Rapids, Michigan, 2005.

J Pearsall, W Trumble, eds. Oxford English Reference Dictionary. Oxford, England, 2002.

JB Lightfoot. Saint Paul's Epistle to the Galatians. MacMillan, 1900.

E H Peterson. The Message// Remix. Nav Press Publishing Group. Colorado Springs, Colorado, 2003.

DW Riley. My Soul Looks Back, Lest I Forget. Harper/Collins, New York, 1995.

AT Robertson. New Testament Word Pictures: Galatians.

JRW Stott. The Message of Galatians. The Bible Speaks Today series. Inter-Varsity Press, Leicester, England, 1968.

JRW Stott. Issues Facing Christians Today, 4th Edition. Zondervan Publishing House, Grand Rapids, Michigan, 2005.

VD Verbrugge. The NIV Theological Dictionary of New Testament Words.Zondervan Publishing House, Grand Rapids, Michigan, 2000.

A Whyte. Bible Characters: New Testament. Oliphants Ltd. London, England, 1953.

WW Wiersbe. Be Free – Galatians. Victor Books, Wheaton, Illinois, 1975.

M Zerwick, M Grosvenor. A Grammatical Analysis of the New
Testament Editrice Pontifico Istituto Biblico, Rome 1993

CHAPTER HEADINGS.

1.
OUTLINE OF GALATIANS
CHAPTER ONE.

Paul, whose apostleship stems from the risen Christ, and God the Father, and his Christian brothers, write to the churches in Galatia.

He wants grace and peace to flow out to them from God the Father, and the Lord Jesus Christ, whose self-giving sacrifice was aimed at rescue, is in line with God's will, and merits eternal glory.

Paul is amazed at the speed of their defection from the call and grace of Christ to a different gospel which is no real alternative. They are victims of trouble-makers and perverters of the Gospel. Paul pronounces an anathema, and repeats it, on anyone, including himself, who preaches another gospel. Paul is no plausible men-pleaser (like the false teachers), but an authentic servant of Christ.

No human agent invented, or passed on, informally or formally, the Gospel Paul preached. It was a message revealed by Jesus Christ. Paul's past life in Judaism was that of a fierce persecutor and destroyer of God's church. He was a 'fast-track' mover within Judaism, but has now obeyed the God who separated him since birth, and graciously called him to preach Christ among non-Jews. Paul did not take human advice, or consult the Jerusalem apostles, but headed for Arabia and Damascus.

There was a three-year interval before he visited Jerusalem. The visit lasted only two weeks, and he linked up with Peter and James only. The solemn truth is that he went to Syria and Silicia, and was personally unknown, but he was a source of praise to God among the churches of Judea, because he, the persecutor, had turned preacher.

CHAPTER 1

PAUL THE BOY,
THE MAN AND THE APOSTLE.
Galatians 1 verses 1-2.

I want to give some sort of explanation of the New Testament letter written by the apostle Paul to the Galatians. I would suggest that you have your Bible or New Testament beside you, open at Galatians. It might be an idea to have a notebook and pen or pencil....Apart from my occasional inconsequential meanderings, most of what I write will be related to this letter, and in this chapter we have a modest aim: to talk about the man who wrote the letter, and look his description of himself in chapter 1 verses 1 and 2 : 'Paul, an apostle - sent not from men, nor by man, but by Jesus Christ and God the Father, who raised him from the dead – and all the brothers with me, to the churches in Galatia.'

Have you ever listened in to someone else's telephone conversation? Sometimes we can't help it, but in these days of mobile phones, people don't seem to mind, especially on buses. Reading one of these New Testament letters is a bit like eavesdropping. It is so one-sided that you start wondering about what kind of person is at the receiving end of the call, and then speculating about the person who is doing the talking. Like Keyhole Kate in the comics I used to read, it is easy to get things wrong, and so we should try to set the record straight about Paul and try to discover where Galatia was and what was the specific bit of bother that led Paul to write such a cracker of a letter? It sparkles and crackles for only 149 verses – a relatively short letter for Paul – but goes for the jugular on a lot of important issues. It deals with Christian authority, and true and false apostles. It addresses the questions 'What is the Gospel? Are we saved by sacraments and a sacrificing priesthood? Is Jesus and His grace enough or is there something else we should be doing? What use is the Old Testament? How can we agree AND DISAGREE as Christian brothers?', and issues like alienation and belonging, the relationship between law and grace, and faith and works. This is bang up-to-date stuff!

What kind of person was Paul, boy and man? What kind of people are we? Those who study these things say that there are three factors which make us what we are – heredity, environment, and instinct. On the hereditary side, we inherit things like our eye colour, hair colour, and physical frame from our parents. Our genetic inheritance may influence our intellectual or artistic abilities. On the environment side, if we are well-nourished, our brains as well as our bodies can grow normally. If we are well-taught, we can realise our potential and ambitions, and avoid mental frustration. Good play opportunities and a rich mixture of opportunities to relate can help our social development. Good parental models in the spiritual realm can influence us towards God in such a way that the Bible proverb comes true in us: 'Train up a child in the way that he should go, and when he is old he will not depart from it'. In the instinct department, the strength of our self-preservation instinct can separate the cautious from the risk-takers. We know that Freud based his psychological theories on a limited sample (neurotic women), but one general truth of the Freudians holds good, that healthy physical and emotional relationships with our parents in childhood will result in a healthy adult, able to relate well to others.
What about Paul? In some ways he was what the Americans call a crazy mixed-up kid, a hotch-potch of Jewish, Roman and Greek influence. The first part of the amalgam was the **Jewish** element. His parents were part of the Jewish Diaspora, the scattered settlements of Jews throughout the Mediterranean world. Paul later describes his home town Tarsus as 'no mean city'. It was reckoned to have about half a million people living there in Roman times. It lay about 15 kilometres inland from the Asia Minor coast, and a major road led from there through the Cilician Gates, a famous pass through the Taurus Mountains about 50 kilometres distant. In the Philippian letter, Paul, the little one, or 'the wee man', (Hebrew name Sha'ul or Saul) says he was a 'Hebrew of the Hebrews'. We usually interpret

this as 'the Hebrew son of Hebrew-speaking parents.' He was strictly orthodox, 'circumcised the eighth day', and would be taken to the synagogue services, and inculcated into Judaism, which is of course a way of life rather than an intellectual or ritual discipline. After his Bar-mitsvah, no matter how clever he was, he would be taught a practical skill, in his case tent-making, which prepared any Jew for the uncertainties of living in a hostile pagan environment. If he could not make his living with his brains, he could always make money using his hands. He made swift, committed and ambitious progress in Judaism, and was sent to Jerusalem with the cream of the crop, to study under Rabbi Gamaliel. Paul became a Pharisee, one of the spiritual descendants of the Hasidim of the Maccabaean period, a specialist student of the Torah, or Old Testament Law.

There were about 6000 Pharisees in Israel at this period. They met in lunch-clubs, swopped stories and sayings by scholarly authorities, and believed God Himself spent some hours per day studying the Torah. They believed that if they could persuade the general public to keep the Law for only one day, then their hoped-for Messiah or Deliverer would come.

The second part of the amalgam in his character was the **Roman** element. The Mediterranean world in Paul's time was dominated by the Colossus of the Roman Empire. Paul was a Roman citizen by birth, one of three ways of obtaining it. The other two ways were by purchase, or by grant for services rendered to the Roman State. Tarsus had passed under Roman control as a result of Pompey's conquests, and it became the capital of Cilicia in 67 BC. Some scholars have made the interesting but unsubstantiated deduction from Paul's trade as a tent-maker that his father may have been a supplier of tents to the Roman Army, and obtained citizenship by grant. Another secondary by-product is that Paul was the first son in the family, since the eldest sons in Jewish families generally followed the father's trade.

The **Greek** influences on Paul were very strong. Alexander the Great had saved Tarsus being burned down by the retreating Persians in 333 BC. Tarsus was a university town, and a show-piece of Alexander's policy of 'polis-planting'. (this has nothing to do with the strategy of Glasgow's chief constable! – in Glasgow a policeman is called a 'polis') Polis means city in Greek, and Alexander's plan was a combination of brain-washing and ethnic cleansing for subject states. Veterans and wounded soldiers from Alexander's army were encouraged to settle down, marry the local girls, and spread the taste and influence of Greek culture. Cities were established with baths, gymnasia, libraries, a stadium, hippodrome and theatre. The culture of body and mind flourished under a Greek parasol, so to speak. In language terms, Greek was the lingua franca of the Mediterranean world, rather like English is today. Paul was thoroughly familiar with the Septuagint, a Greek translation of the Old Testament, made in Egypt in the third century BC. The New Testament was written mainly in Koine Greek, which used to be regarded as almost 'the language of angels', until they discovered it was the language of the people, common Greek, a simplified form of classical Greek. It is always interesting to think about what makes people what they are. In my own case, I was the child of a Roman Catholic mother who gave up her faith to marry my father, who would have called himself a 'Presbyterian atheist'. I was born out of due time, the natural child of my parents over fifteen years after my mother was told she could not have children, born when she was in her forties. At an ordinary State school in Possil, Glasgow, I had the best teachers possible, and during my time in London my tutors were world-class scholars, and I was privileged to hear world-class preachers in London churches in the 1960s, people like John Stott and Martyn Lloyd-Jones. I am sure many of you reading this could quietly bow your head and thank God today for a tremendous heritage, good homes, and in some cases good Christian parents who were praying for you before you were born.

When Paul was an adult, he, like some of us, had a life-changing experience of the Lord Jesus Christ. The Roman Catholic theologian Ronald Knox says 'Beware of a man with an experience!' When Paul was a fully-fledged Pharisee, a top dog in Rabbinic Judaism, he had this experience which changed his whole life. Paul at this time probably shared the Jewish view of Jesus of Nazareth as a blasphemous upstart from Nazareth a 'you've got to be kidding' kind of town, who was too young to speak with authority, (Jesus was in his early thirties when he died), and who had not had his training through the appropriate channels in Jerusalem. He also did not resort to the Rabbinic style of teaching through quoting the authorities. The most annoying feature about Jesus was that he was a brilliant debater who could spring any traps set for him by his opponents, **and he always spoke with authority**...Jews believed that Jesus had got his just desserts from the Romans as a result of a Jewish conspiracy to get rid of him. Although he had been crucified as a criminal, there were persistent rumours by the followers of the (Jesus) Way that he had risen from the dead and was alive. Paul worked tirelessly for the Jewish authorities, systematically hounding and rounding up the followers of Jesus. Paul had actually been present at the stoning of Stephen the first Christian martyr, and agreed with all that was going on that day.

One day on the way to Damascus, Paul was confronted by the risen Christ, who made it clear to him that it wasn't the Christians he was persecuting, but the Christ. 'Saul, Saul, why are you persecuting ME?' The dazzling vision of Christ temporarily blinded Paul, and he was helped by the believers in Jesus in Damascus, and was never the same again. All the ideas of the brilliant young Pharisee were thrown into the melting-pot, and he was reshaped into becoming God's chosen messenger to the non-Jewish, or Gentile nations. Modern terminology would say Paul had made a commitment to Christ. Older Christians would say he had been converted or changed or saved, and had become a born-again believer. Whatever the accuracy of the terminology, it is the experience that counts. God meets and changes people in a variety of different ways. Some open up to Christ gently and quietly like a flower opening to the sunlight, like Lydia the dealer in purple dye in Acts 18 . Others come in a spectacular crisis experience, like the jailor in Acts 18. Some of us have shared in some way the conversion experience of Paul. It gradually or suddenly dawned on us that Jesus did not simply die for the whole world in general, but for us in particular. We repented of our sins, and believed in Jesus for salvation and forgiveness and new life, and we've never been the same since.

A famous American baseball player, Billy Sunday, was asked how he could be so sure of his experience of conversion. He said 'I was there when it happened, and I ought to know!' Have you had an experience like this? Perhaps today God is calling you to repent and believe in the Lord Jesus Christ. When you take your first stumbling step towards him, you'll find Him running to meet you ...

After a period of retreat in Arabia and Damascus, Paul found a new direction in life when he and his friend Barnabas were sent out on mission by the believers in the Christian church in Syrian Antioch. His three missionary journeys, and careful missionary strategy, took him to key cities in Asia Minor and Greece, which would serve in future years as nucleating centres for Good News outreach.

One of these areas was called 'Galatia', and much ink has been spilt trying to figure out exactly what Paul meant when he wrote to 'the churches in Galatia'(chapter 1 verse 2). The name 'Galatia' is derived from Gaul, the ancient name for France, because a group from Gaul had settled there in the third century BC. The issue is whether Paul is writing to ethnic Galatia or provincial Galatia. Ethnic Galatia was located in the **North** of Asia Minor. The Roman province of Galatia was extended to include towns in the South which Paul visited in his first missionary journey – Pisidian Antioch (to distinguish it from Syrian Antioch), Iconium, Lystra and Derbe (Acts 13-14).

I share the view taken by some reputable scholars that Paul is referring **to South Galatia,** which has two important spin-offs. First of all, this means that Galatians could be the earliest book in the New Testament, written before the Council of Jerusalem in AD 49 (Acts 15), and, secondly, the area could have been the place where Paul got his famous 'thorn in the flesh', some physical, debilitating ailment which Paul refers to in his Corinthian letters. There was a spiritual dimension to his pain, for Paul calls the thorn in the flesh 'a messenger of Satan'.

South Galatia was a swampy area rife with mosquitoes, and some take the view that Paul's thorn in the flesh was malaria, a recurrent nuisance to all those who have contracted it. John Moncrieffe, my history teacher at school, used to be off for several days each year with malaria. He had served in the Far East during the war and caught the disease there.

Paul had no sooner established some groups of believers in churches in the area, than guess what? The false teachers arrived like terriers snapping at his heels, and launched a two-pronged attack, first of all attacking his status and authority as an apostle. Although we have to surmise what was going at the other end, rather like deducing the other end of a telephone conversation, the kind of thing they were saying was : Who is this Paul, anyway? He wasn't one of the original twelve disciples of Jesus, was he? Was he not a vicious persecutor of Christians? Who gave him authority to establish churches?

The second prong of the attack was more subtle : They did not deny what he had taught the Galatian believers, but their approach that his message was good as far as it went, but in addition to believing in Jesus, new converts had to be circumcised as a sign of their covenant with God, and would have to follow the Jewish calendar and Jewish food laws, to complete their commitment...

When Paul heard about this, he wrote in what Leith Samuel called 'white hot urgency'. The archaeologists who worked on papyrus letters discovered on Egyptian rubbish dumps have discovered there was a set template or pattern for letter-writing in the ancient world. There was usually a greeting, followed by a prayer for the good health of the recipients. There was a thanksgiving (usually to pagan gods). Then there was the special content of the letter, with its main news. Finally there were special regards and personal greetings. Practically every one of Paul's letters shows this exact pattern – except Galatians! Paul gets ripped in right away! He does what the British Lions' rugby coach told them on the way to New Zealand: 'Retaliate first!' Paul does not pussy-foot about here. He immediately sets out his credentials as the risen Christ's apostle with divine authority from God Himself. 'Paul, an apostle – sent not from men nor by man, but by Jesus Christ and God the Father, who raised him from the dead.'

'Apostle' was not a general word like 'believer', saint' or 'brother'. It was a special description reserved for the Twelve disciples of

Jesus, and for one or two others appointed by the risen Lord (for example. James the Lord's brother). Therefore there can be no apostolic succession except that of a total loyalty to the apostolic doctrine of the New Testament. The apostles had no successors. They were unique in two ways – first of all, in their link with the risen Christ, and secondly, in their link to the formation of the New Testament, which took shape during their lifetime.

Paul is therefore claiming to belong to a very select group, distinct from 'all the brothers who are with me' (chapter 1 verse 2), and elsewhere he argues that the risen Christ appeared to him as to one born out of due time. His vision of the risen Christ on the Damascus Road qualified him to be ranked with the Twelve.

Usually in Paul's letters, he is content to describe himself as 'Paul, called to be an apostle.' Here in Galatians, he is stressing that his apostleship is intrinsically divine, not from men by human appointment, nor by man by human commission.

Some modern authorities are at pains to regard themselves as witnesses on the same level playing-field as the first century apostles. In fact, because Jesus said 'you shall do greater works than these' their signature tune would seem to be 'anything you can do, I can do better.'

Another school of thought is that the church wrote the Bible, but the New Testament writers like Paul wrote as apostles of Christ, not the church. Some would hold that the grace of God flows through church-approved conduits only, that is through the succession of appointed members of a church hierarchy. It is interesting that four of the words used for God's leaders are, firstly 'apostle' or 'sent one' from the Greek word apostello to send, or, secondly, 'herald' or, thirdly, 'ambassador' or fourthly, 'teacher', none of which has intrinsic authority. Their authority comes from outside themselves, from God through Christ. That is why we can trust what they wrote.

In the next chapter we will turn our spotlight away from Paul the man to Paul's message, from the authority of his role to the content of his Gospel.

QUESTIONS FOR DISCUSSION.
1 V 1-2

1. What are the advantages/disadvantages of writing letters?

2. In today's 'fast-track' world, has 'texting' replaced letter-writing? Is this a good thing?

3. Paul's background affected his later life. Discuss any way in which you can trace God's hand in your childhood?

4. Paul obviously believed God activated his call to Christian service.
    Was that confined to Paul's time, or are there 'apostles' in the same sense today?

5. Is 'people of the resurrection' an accurate or misleading description for Christians. Can you think of another one?

CHAPTER 2.

PAUL'S MESSAGE, GENERAL AND PARTICULAR.
Galatians Chapter 1 v3-5.

In the last chapter we had a look at the first phase of the two-pronged attack on the Galatian believers, the questioning of Paul's authority as an apostle. The attack was launched by the false teachers who dogged Paul's steps. We looked at Paul as boy and man and apostle, and saw that he was a lively mixture of Roman, Greek and Jewish influences. When he was an enthusiastic attacker of the followers of the Way of Jesus, he had a special confrontation with the Risen Jesus, who stopped him in his tracks on the road to Damascus. He realised he was persecuting the Christ rather than the Christians, and his life was dramatically changed, like the lives of countless thousands since. In the opening passage of Galatians, Paul defends his authority to be an apostle on the grounds that, like the Twelve disciples of Jesus, he too had seen Jesus face to face, and his call to be an apostle did not spring from popular vote nor a personal leader in the church, but directly from Jesus the Messiah and God the Father. Have you ever thought that such intimate contact with God can be a reality in your life? Isn't it amazing that God, the Gentle Giant of the universe, could become our Friend?

In this chapter, we see how Paul switched from defending himself to defending the message he brought. Eugene Peterson wrote: 'When men and women get their hands on religion, one of the first things they often do is turn it into an instrument for controlling others, either putting them or keeping them in their place. The history of such religious manipulation is long and tedious.
'In his early travels, Paul founded a series of churches in the Roman Province of Galatia. A few years later, Paul learned

that religious leaders of the old school had come into these churches, called his views and authority into question, and were re-introducing the old ways, herding all those freedom-loving Christians back into the corral of religious rules and regulations.'

We have noted in the past that religion can be a kind of whitewash, an external and superficial cover-up, and that what some folk want is an inoculation of religion to prevent them ever catching the real thing! The heart of the Christian gospel is our relationship with God through faith in what the Lord Jesus has done, not a set of rules and regulations.

When Paul heard what the false teachers were up to, he was livid! He was angry with the old guard for their bully-boy tactics, and he was angry with some Christians for keeling over before this onslaught. It's good for us to see that Paul had red blood in his veins, and produced in this letter a call directing them and us to our Christian birthright to freedom. Peterson says 'Freedom is a delicate gift, easily perverted and often squandered.' The Message translation of today's section says:

'So I greet you with the great words, grace and peace! We know the meaning of those words because Jesus Christ rescued us from this evil world we're in by offering Himself as a sacrifice for our sins. God's plan is that we all experience that rescue. Glory to God forever! Oh, Yes!'

This is all exciting stuff, and as this chapter unfolds, we'll unpack the content of Paul's message. Stay with us! Read on!

Many of today's people , young and old, are on a spiritual search for reality in God. In this chapter we're looking at the heart of Paul's Message, which he was ready to defend 'with jackets off' as the Glaswegians say, against all-comers. I see five elements in this message, when we separate it out: Are you ready?!

The first one is **God's Overflowing Grace.** 'the great word grace'

The second one is **God's Indwelling Peace.** 'the great word peace'

The third one is **Christ's Glorious Deliverance**. 'Jesus Christ rescued us from this evil world we're in'

The fourth element is **Christ's Unique Sacrifice.** 'by offering Himself as a sacrifice for our sins.'

The fifth one is **The Father and Son's Glorious Plan.** 'God's plan is that we all experience that rescue. Glory to God forever! Oh, Yes!'

What does this great word Grace mean? As I have written elsewhere, grace is a sunshine word. It is the free, undeserved and unearned favour from God. Paul writes in Ephesians 2 verses 7 -9: ' Now God has us where he wants us, with all the time in this world and the next to shower grace and kindness upon is in Christ Jesus. Saving is all His idea, and all His work. All we do is trust Him enough to let Him do it. It is God's gift from start to finish! We don't play the major role. If we did, we'd probably go around bragging that we'd done the whole thing. No, we neither make or save ourselves. God does both the making and the saving.'

God's grace has a halo of beauty around it, emanating from a generous-hearted God. In the Roman world, it signified the Emperor's bounty as he distributed largesse on his accession or birthday. In a Christian sense, it is God's gift of eternal life mediated through the self-giving of Christ on the Cross. Paul contrasts wages and gifts in Romans chapter 10 verse 9 : 'For the wages of sin is death, but the gift of God is eternal life through Jesus Christ our Lord.'

Let me use two illustrations of gracious treatment from the Bible, one from each Testament. The first one is the Old Testament story of David and Mephibosheth in the second book of Samuel, chapter 9. Mephibosheth was the crippled son of David's dead friend Jonathan. When David the shepherd-boy became king, he sought out any surviving member of Saul's family to honour them for Jonathan's sake. We should point out that the normal reason for this sort of search was to wipe out any potential opposition. Therefore, it is understandable that when Mephibosheth is brought into David's presence, David reassures him that he wants to do something special for him for Jonathan's sake. David showers him with kindness, and we are told that 'Mephibosheth ate at the king's table, just like one of the royal family.' God's grace is like that. He delights to shower

His kindness on a shower of spiritual cripples like us.

The New Testament illustration is taken from Jesus' Parable of the Two Wasters in Luke's Gospel chapter 15, better known as 'The Parable of the Prodigal Son.' A farmer's younger son demands his inheritance money in advance and leaves home, squanders it in profligate living, and finishes up working as a pig-man (the ultimate disgrace for a Jew). In the blackness of his personal pigsty, he made up his mind to return home, and rehearsed the script of what he would say to his father.

Jesus said: 'When he was still a long way off, his father saw him. His heart pounding, he ran out, embraced him, and kissed him.' Celebration was the order of the day, and Jesus obviously meant us to picture God like the father in the story, running to meet us and shower us with kindness when we take the first faltering steps towards Him.

Paul says in Romans 'We can understand a person dying for a person worth dying for, and we can understand how someone good and noble could inspire us to selfless sacrifice. But God put His love on the line for us by offering His Son in sacrificial death while we were of no use whatever to Him.' An old acrostic on the word grace defines it as 'God's Riches At Christ's Expense.' Now we shall consider that other great word 'Peace'.

In this chapter, we are taking the theme 'Born Free' from Galatians chapter 1 verses 3 to 5, and I pray that God will bless us through this encounter.. Now we're going to spend a few minutes to consider this great word 'peace', and think about God's Indwelling Peace. Paul greeted the Galatians with grace and peace, which was a double whammy blessing from both sides of the stable, grace being the Greek expression, and peace the Hebrew blessing. The Greek word for peace is 'eirene', hence the girl's name Irene. Eirene had a kind of negative meaning of absence of war, but the Hebrew word for peace is 'shalom' , which opens up rich vistas of meaning when we invest the New Testament word with the Old Testament meaning. Shalom can mean peace, well-being, completeness, welfare, soundness, harmony or agreement. It can mean material prosperity or physical safety. In Jesus' time, or in Israel today, shalom can be used as a conventional greeting. But Jesus took this conventional mould and filled it with a new content for His disciples.   In John's Gospel chapter 14 and verse 27 Jesus said : 'I'm leaving you well and whole. That's my parting gift to you. Peace. I don't leave you the way you're used to being left – feeling abandoned, bereft. So don't be upset. Don't be distraught.' I think Jesus meant that His peace was a positive, special gift, not merely a conventional greeting.

The world we live in is in turmoil. We never can predict what mayhem is about to erupt in our world. Nationally, Britain is not a nation at peace. Militarily, there are dirty little wars going on in Iraq and Afghanistan, with daily carnage and misery. Socially and medically we are in a state. The number of prescriptions issued in Britain associated with stress and depression have doubled in the past 10 years. Sexually transmitted infections are raging at a rate, especially among our young people, which makes a laughing-stock of the State approach to sex education. They seem to be trying to put the fire out by throwing petrol at it. We have the highest teenage pregnancy rate in Europe, huge alcohol, drug and violence problems in our inner cities, so that there are no-go areas all over the land. Our rate of credit card debt is said to have levelled off a little, but we are a nation of debtors and insomniacs. Marriage and family break-up is at such a level that we will only be able to assess the damage a few decades ahead. Tony Blair's brave New Labour may drown swimming in the same kind of sleaze that toppled the Old Tories just a few years ago.

Perhaps as you are reading all this, you may be able to grunt agreement that some of these things are close to you or your home, or family. Is there no good news? Yes there is! Jesus came to bring us peace. That peace, like anything worthwhile, was bought at great cost. Christ died on a Calvary's hill to bring peace through the blood of His cross. That peace with God comes through the removal of our sinful enmity and rebellion against God. The Christian way is not escapism; it is realism. We can look at our world full-frontal and engage with all its problems with a mind at ease and a heart at peace with God, and find incidentally that there are horizontal spin-offs to a correct vertical relationship with God. When we are at peace with God, our relationships with others should improve. Paul wanted Christ's peace to be a built-in feature of the Galatian believers' new-found freedom. This directs our attention to look at Christ's Glorious Deliverance.

The theme 'Born Free' is a good slogan for a study of Galatians, and in these opening verses Paul highlights Christ's Glorious Deliverance by saying 'Christ rescued us from this evil world we're in'. The New Testament talks a lot about personal salvation. The Good News of Jesus Christ is that He came to deliver us from darkness to light, from the power of Satan to the peace of God. The psalmist in Psalm 40 says : 'He lifted me out of the ditch, pulled me from deep mud. He stood me up on a solid rock to make sure I wouldn't slip.' As you know, I much prefer the idea of relationship to the idea of religion, but Christianity is a rescue religion based on the great deeds of a Person. Jesus is a Saviour, a Rescuer, a Deliverer, the great Emancipator from the bondage of sin. The verb translated 'rescued' here is a strong verb, used of rescuing the Jews from the slavery of Egypt, of the rescue of Peter from prison, and of the rescue of Paul from an angry lynch mob. It is as if Jesus has snatched us from the jaws of death, and that is an encouraging and uplifting thought. In relation to the Lord's deliverance of Jerusalem, Zechariah says : 'Surprise! Everything is going up in flames, but I reach in and pull out Jerusalem!'. We used to sing a song in Lambhill Mission 'He rescued me His own to be, a brand from the burning he set me free. Oh, how I'll praise Him for eternity, a brand from the burning He rescued me.'

This is a novel idea. A church is not so much a hospital for the spiritually wounded, or a social club for people who like to play silly games, as a rescue shop for those in danger of losing salvation, in this evil age in which we live. Christians are not taken out of the world, like the people zapped away to another time zone in Star Trek or Doctor Who. Christians are placed by God in the world to give hope, and shed light, and be salt. Christians have inherited the Jewish idea of the two ages – ha-olam ha-zzeh, this age, and ha-olam habba', the coming age. Christians are rescued so that they may live in this evil age life which displays the quality of the life to come. They are like salmon swimming against the current to the spawning grounds, onward and upward, an exhausting but a rewarding lifestyle. We are forgiven and rescued, set free to experience eternal life, here and now! What a mind-blowing picture...Would you not like to be involved in all this? One of the ladies in our church had a car sticker which said: 'Carpenter needs joiners!' We've looked at grace and peace and deliverance.

The theme is 'Born Free', the book is Galatians, the message is Paul's defence of his gospel or Good News, and the feature is from Galatians 1 verse 4 'Jesus offered Himself as a sacrifice for our sins.' John Stott wrote in his lucid way: 'the death of Jesus Christ was neither a display of love, nor an example of heroism, but a sacrifice for sin.'....'The New Testament teaches that Christ's death was a sin-offering, the unique sacrifice by which our sins may be forgiven and put away.'

The Jews in the Old Testament period had a rich vocabulary and a daily experience of the effects of sin. To summarise the range of meaning of the Hebrew words for sin it is a **deficiency,** a coming short of God's glory, it is a **deviation** from the path of God's will for our lives, it is a series of acts of **disobedience** against God's commandments, and it is **defiance**, a metaphorical shaking of our fist at God, and refusing to have Him controlling our lives. The human predicament cannot be solved by throwing money at it by building better houses, schools or hospitals. Our sad hearts cannot be cured by pills or pleasure. The big issue for any one of us is the issue of our sin. We are polluted and defeated and without strength. In Jonathan Swift's book 'Gulliver's Travels' the king of Brobdingnag says to Gulliver : 'I cannot but conclude the bulk of your natives to be the most pernicious race of odious vermin that Nature ever suffered to crawl upon the surface of the earth.'

To the Jews of the Old Testament God's law enshrined in the Ten Commandments was like a mirror to show them their defilement, and the sacrificial system was like soap and water, cleansing them from this pollution. The acrid smell of burning flesh, the smoke over their camp, the rivers of animal blood, were constant reminders of sin.

The New Testament Gospel tells us that it was when we were still without strength that Christ died for the ungodly. His death was special in several ways. First of all it was a **voluntary act.** For all of us, death is the necessary and inevitable outcome of sin. But if Jesus was what Martin Luther called 'God's proper man', neither superhuman nor subhuman, but the only real human who ever lived the way God intended, then He did not deserve to die. For us death is a necessary fruit; for Jesus death was a voluntary act. He gave His life for us. Secondly, it was a **unique sacrifice.** The death of Jesus was qualitatively superior to the death of any of the sacrificial victims of Old Testament times. The Letter to the Hebrews in the New Testament uses the words hapax or ephapax in Greek, meaning 'once for all' or 'definitely once for all', dispensing with the need for any more animal sacrifice. The writer also says that when He completed the finished work of our salvation Jesus sat down, because the work was done. There were thousands of people crucified during the period of the Roman Empire. But this crucifixion was different. He died for our sins. Peter says 'He carried our sins in His own body on the lump of wood.' Thirdly His death was special because it was a **substitutionary death.** He died in my place, instead of me, as my substitute, taking on Himself the awful penalty of my sin. In the glorious Old Testament chapter Isaiah 53, the prophet writes : 'all we like sheep have gone astray, we have turned each one to his own way, but the Lord has laid on Him the iniquity of us all.' He did not come to dazzle us with His glory but to save us by His grace.

Christ's mind-set took Him to self-humiliation, obedience to God the Father's will, and an excruciatingly painful death, because He loved us. John chapter 3 and verse 16 says: 'God so loved the world that he gave His one and only Son that whoever believes on Him should not perish but have everlasting life.' We cannot explain God's love, but it is gloriously possible to experience it for ourselves.

Paul was answering the old guard of false teachers by setting out the exact boundary lines of his message, and the final act in the drama of salvation is in verses 4 and 5, that all that Jesus did for us when He died for us was 'according to the will of our God and Father.' 'Glory to God forever! Oh Yes!' The message seems to be that God the Father and Jesus Christ were hand and glove in the whole business! Paul says in his Corinthian letters 'God was in Christ, reconciling the world to Himself.' In other words the drama of what some scholars call 'the Christ-event' was not haphazard. It was the culmination of all the hopes and prophecies for centuries. Alex Vidler argues that the Cross was the fulcrum of world history, with all of the Old Testament revelation leading up to this climax, and even the final judgement looking back to it, for men will be judged on their response to Christ's great work on the Cross. From the point of view of Christ's life, His death was not a tragic accident, nor the result of a human conspiracy, but a triumphant finale (with His resurrection) to what God has to say to us. And Father and Son have acted in agreement to a design or plan that this may happen. No wonder Paul finishes up with a doxology!

What we have wrapped up in these opening five verses of Galatians is what modern descriptions call 'a package'. Christ died for our sins to rescue us. God the Father and Jesus Christ His Son appointed Paul as an apostle and witness to all this. Those who believe experience and enjoy the gifts of grace and peace, deliverance and freedom which the Lord Jesus Christ has won for us. That is all! Is that not enough? Is it enough for you? It wasn't for some folk, as we'll see, if you can stay with us into the next phase...

QUESTIONS FOR DISCUSSION.
1 v 3-5

1. What is so amazing about the grace of God?

2. What is so distinctive about the peace of God?

3. Chapter 1 v 1 and chapter 1 v 3 link God the Father and Jesus Christ the Son as working together in God's call to Paul, and His blessing on the Galatians. Why should we keep them together in our thinking?

4. Find THREE activities of the Lord Jesus Christ on our behalf in 1 v 4. Are these central in our idea of the Gospel?

CHAPTER 3

TURNCOATS AND TROUBLE-MAKERS
Galatians chapter 1 verses 6-10.

In the first few verses of Galatians chapter 1, the apostle Paul defended his status as an apostle, claiming that he was especially and divinely called by God the Father and the risen Christ, and sent out on a divine mission. He was responding to false teachers who had rubbished his character and credentials. Paul broke all the conventional patterns the ancient world had for letter-writing in order to retaliate against the old guard of false teachers. They attacked not only Paul's status as an apostle, but also his message, and their attack was really quite subtle and oblique. They undermined Paul's message by saying it was good as far as it went, but it was incomplete. As well as believing on Jesus and His Gospel, they argued that the Galatians would have to complete their commitment by being circumcised, observing the Jewish calendar, and keeping Jewish food laws! Paul was livid, and very strongly set out his stall that God's way of salvation was by grace alone, through faith alone, and had as its sole and central teaching God's gifts of overflowing grace and indwelling peace, Christ's glorious deliverance, His unique sacrifice, and the combined resources of the Father and Son's glorious plan for the life of each believer. End of Story! Can you understand how Paul felt? Have you ever been rubbished as a person by workmates or so-called friends? Have you ever had your expression of your plans and ideas ridiculed and criticised? You can perhaps understand the situation...It was as if he had handed these prisoners of sin in Galatia a 'get out of jail' ticket, and as they came out of the main gate, the old guards headed them off and herded them back into their prison cells! Paul's reaction is not based only on defending his own personal standpoint or viewpoint. He is sensitive for the glory of the Lord Jesus Christ and His Gospel. He was also keen to protect the new-found freedom in Christ that the Galatian believers had experienced.

Paul's response to the false teachers in today's section of Galatians is pretty strong stuff. Here it is in Eugene Peterson's paraphrase The Message:

'I can't believe your fickleness – how easily you have turned traitor to him who called you by the grace of Christ by embracing a variant message! It is not a minor variation, you know, it is completely other, an alien message, a no-message, a lie about God. Those who are provoking this agitation among you are turning the message of Christ on its head. Let me be blunt. If one of us – even if an angel from heaven- were to preach something other than what we preached originally, let him be cursed. I said it once, I'll say it again. If anyone, regardless of reputation or credentials, preaches something other than what you received originally, let him be cursed.'

After I left school, I was a student apprentice metallurgist, and spent five years with Colvilles Limited, iron and steel makers, in the days when Scotland had a steel industry. I felt very privileged in Clyde Ironworks blast furnace lab to be asked to make up the standard solutions used for titrations in chemical analysis. To the smart boys today, it would be reckoned 'bucket chemistry', but never mind, it worked. We had to make up a large quantity of potassium dichromate, for example, and when it was made up I had to measure the estimation against British standard metals and adjust if necessary until my solutions were a perfect match of the contents printed on the British Standard metal samples. Nearly all our lab results depended on these standard solutions being spot-on, accurately made up. Any one who messed about with the standard solutions was heading for a P45 and the works gate...

This is what it was like for the believers in the churches Paul established. These superstitious pagans were prisoners of fear and guilt and sin, like so many in modern-day Britain. Paul had given them a perfect solution which would make them free. They were utterly incapable of finding deliverance. Even if they lived perfectly for the rest of their lives, their past would still haunt them in their dreams and in their waking hours. Witch-doctors, fortune tellers, and potions could never deal with their past or change their lives in the present or for the future. The gods they believed in were fickle, cruel and immoral. Then along came Paul to tell them that the God who created them also loved them, so much that He sent His one and only Son to die, in order to set them free, forgiving their past and guaranteeing their future, if they changed direction, repented and believed in the Lord Jesus. They needn't work their socks off for salvation, it all stemmed from God's grace. Even the faith they exercised to trust Christ was God's gift, because the Holy Spirit of God would kick-start the process which brought them to faith. Their only real contribution to their salvation was their sin, and they couldn't brag about that!

Then along came the false teachers, and like a malicious interferer in our laboratory, they started messing about with the standard solution. They rubbished the qualifications of the chemist, and claimed that the procedures were inadequate. They argued that the standard solution needed a dash of this and a splash of that... Faith plus a ceremony of circumcision, plus a dash of self-denial to pump up your pride, and so on. No wonder Paul was livid. When they diluted the standard solution, everything went haywire. They were tampering with the grace and glory of God in the Gospel, and were destroying the birthright to freedom which the Galatians had been given...

The world today is a complex place, and people expect to jump through a lot of expensive and time-consuming hoops to find satisfaction and deliverance. The Gospel of the grace of a loving God and His perfect Son, demonstrated in His self-giving sacrifice, is too simple for them. They want to contribute something other than their sin to their salvation, in order to enhance the feel-good factor...They can't agree with the old hymn:

'Nothing in my hand I bring, simply to Thy Cross I cling, naked, look to Thee for dress, helpless, look to Thee for grace, foul I to the fountain fly, wash me Saviour, or I die..'

The letter stands out from Paul's other letters because there is no greeting, prayer, praise or thanks for them. Instead, Paul is amazed at how quickly and how easily they have been knocked out of their stride by false teachers. Then he describes the Galatians very strongly, has a major moan about the false teachers, and pronounces the strongest anathema on those who tamper with the Gospel. He says they have 'turned traitor' by their actions, and substituted the gospel of grace by an alien gospel which is not good news at all. The Greek verb translated 'turned' means 'to change sides'. In West of Scotland culture, it is like someone who was found festooned in Celtic regalia singing Celtic songs in the Celtic stadium one week, is found wearing all the Rangers gear singing Rangers songs the following week! In on the pitch terms, it is like what actually happened - Maurice Johnston swearing one week that Celtic were 'a grand old team', the only team he ever wanted to play for, and the next week he signed for Rangers! In army terms, it is not merely like a deserter, it is someone who is now fighting for his former enemy...Paul is saying that the Galatian believers are spiritual turncoats. They were turning away from the God who had called them in the free grace of Christ, and had become enslaved to a travesty of a gospel, where human effort was added to the gospel of Christ and human merit was added to the merit of Christ.

Another point about the false teachers' gospel was that for the Galatians', it was not just a matter of mistaken theology, it was a matter of misplaced loyalty. They had defected from a Person rather than a position. John Stott writes: 'To turn from the Gospel of grace is to turn from the God of grace. Let the Galatians beware, who have so readily and rashly started turning away. It is impossible to forsake it (the gospel) without forsaking Him (God).'

The effect of all this was that the church was agitato, troubled and unsettled. The false teachers had not only diluted, polluted and corrupted the Gospel, they had reversed it , turned it upside down. John Stott says again 'You cannot modify or supplement the Gospel without radically altering its character.' ..... 'the devil disturbs the church as much by error as by evil. When he cannot entice Christian people into sin, he deceives them with false doctrine.'

When the gospel has been robbed of its inherent power, it loses its attraction and interest. No wonder Paul was amazed and upset.

Paul was so indignant about the false teachers that he pronounced a double anathema on them. Now we have to look at this in some detail. Is this a teacher so jealous of his position that he puts a curse on his rivals? Was this a crusty old bachelor so possessive of his converts that he is willing to repeat anathemas over these rivals for their affections?

There are two points we have to make, neither of which waters down the strength of what Paul writes. The first one is that he includes himself, and even heavenly powers, in the anathema, as if the Gospel were the measuring-stick for any preacher, and not vice-versa. Alan Cole comments 'the message validates the messenger'. He is willing to put himself under the curse of God if he distorts the Gospel. He may be thinking of 'angel' in the general sense of 'messenger' here.

The second point is that he repeats the anathema, in case we are mistakenly thinking that it is a petulant outburst. John Brown, commenting in the nineteenth century, said 'this was no excessive, exaggerated statement ...but his calmly formed and unalterable opinion. Paul underlines what he has said in verse 10 where he asks whether he is doing this to win popular applause... 'If my goal was popularity, I wouldn't bother being Christ's slave.'

You probably know the story about the small boy at the dinner-table who was told to eat his prunes, or God would be angry (we should never of course use God as a big stick to beat our children). That night there was a thunderstorm, and the boy was heard going downstairs into the kitchen muttering 'O God, that's some carry-on over a few prunes!' Paul is not arguing about a few theological prunes here. The glory of Christ was at stake. To add to His work, and embellish it with human ceremonies or traditions, is to devalue it. Some think that the reference to an angel related to Jewish belief that the Jewish law was handed down by angels, and the false teachers were using this to strong-arm the Galatians into following Jewish tradition. A few commentators think the reference to the angel is a hint about Satanic activity, undermining the need for the Cross alone as our way of salvation. All of this raises huge issues about the church in today's world... but we'll leave that until later.

In the section we have been dealing with, the apostle Paul has been giving the Galatian Christians a bit of stick for keeling over so soon after false teachers arrived, and has been pronouncing anathemas on false teachers for distorting the Gospel so that it bears no resemblance to the real thing, and unsettling the churches by tampering with the Gospel. This raises the whole question of whether there is only one Gospel, and how we should react to those who differ from us, in the light of some people's reaction to Paul's writing here as an intemperate outburst. A lot depends on our attitude to Scripture. If we believe that the Bible contains the Word of God rather than is the Word of God, and that we can dismiss some of the Bible's teaching as culturally irrelevant to today's church, then there is no problem. What we have here is a cultural hangover from an intolerant first century missionary. In a former generation strong contrasts were drawn between 'the simple Gospel of Jesus', and the writings of Paul, so that they wrote about the Jesus of History in the Gospels and the Christ of Faith in the Pauline letters. Some would say if we believe this stuff, we are putting Christianity into a first century strait-jacket, and that in this form it is unacceptable to twenty-first century people. The message of deliverance through Christ's sacrifice on the Cross, His given life and shed blood is a Gospel more suitable to the abattoir than the shopping mall. In our enlightened age, we cannot be as rough as Paul was in his treatment of his opponents. The key words for modern Christians are 'tolerance' and 'accommodation'. There is no obverse side to the coin called God's love which would involve us in ideas of wrath and judgement. Who needs the Bible when we can contemplate nature with enlightened minds? 'Comprehend God in all things, for God is in all things. Every single creature is full of God, and is a book about God. If I spent enough time with the tiniest creature - even a caterpillar- I would never have to prepare a sermon.' I once met a man who told me the two people he most admired in history were his father, and Jesus, in that order. He said his father was a greater man than Jesus because his father carried a matchbox in his pocket, and if he found a fly at home he would catch it and put it in the matchbox and release it out into the world again.

If, however, we regard the Bible as a divine production, mirroring the nature of Christ as a perfect combination of the human and the divine, then we have to take what Paul says here seriously. There are two words for 'another' in the New Testament. 'allos' means 'another the same as, a replica' and 'heteros' means 'another, distinct from'. Paul uses the word heteros here. Alan Cole says : 'there can only be a distorted gospel, not another gospel'. The gospel of the false teachers was not an alternative Gospel, it was a different Gospel. Paul's Gospel was the Gospel of free grace. The Jewish view was that every good deed won a credit entry in the heavenly ledger. The truth is we can never stockpile enough merit to win God's favour. Martin Luther, the great reformer, said 'good works do not make a good man'. Christ's gospel of grace and peace, based on His rescue of us, his sacrifice for our sin, in harmony with God's plan for our lives is the only gospel.

The Galatian Letter's author, the apostle Paul, was not out to win men's approval, but God's. It was the false teachers who were men-pleasers, trying to convince the Galatian believers that they could be self-satisfied by some human achievement, won by following some ceremonial rite or kow-towing to some human tradition. Wiersbe tells how when Verdi produced his first opera in Florence, the composer stood discreetly in the shadows, and kept his eye on the face of one man in the audience – the great composer Rossini. Guiseppe Verdi was oblivious to everyone else in the crowd; all he craved was a smile on the face of Rossini, the master musician. Similarly, Paul wanted to please his heavenly Master. Paul did not care what insults or slights he had to suffer for the sake of the Gospel. He wasn't looking for men's approval. He wrote in 2 Corinthians 5 verse 9 'We make it our aim... to please Him.'
Paul measured people not by what they wore or what they said, but by how they responded to Christ and His Gospel. Where they assumed positions of leadership and pushed their false teaching at the expense of the Gospel, pretending to be Christians, Paul is uncompromising in his condemnation.
I think we have to measure the anathemas pronounced here in the light of Paul's white-hot love for his Saviour. We must see how Paul behaved elsewhere. He became all things to all men that he might by all means win some. We have to be able to distinguish people and their ideology. In our country now there is a wave of dislike of Islam. Whatever we think of Islamic

teaching, Christians must never be involved in the bitter hatred of Islamic people. Christian missionaries beat their brains out for decades working in countries in the Middle East, with little apparent fruit for their labour. Now look what has happened – we have had an influx of Islamic people into our country, and a significant number of them have had to rethink their views, and some have turned to Christ, and are worshipping in good numbers in our cities. Some are our neighbours or local shop-keepers, whom we can influence for good and for God.......
We now have to consider how we can have fellowship with those who disagree with us.. This will take us to the final section of our third study in Galatians, where we've been looking at Paul's strong reaction to false teaching in his day, denouncing it as no gospel at all, and giving the Galatian Christians a bit of a verbal 'row' for getting involved, and for being led astray by it. He is keen to safeguard their new-found freedom in God's wonderful grace.

Some people think the churches in Britain have become too slack in their approach to people who would not agree with the Gospel outline Paul gives in this opening chapter of Galatians. They argue that in these days of secularism and humanism Christians of any sort have to get together, and keep together, and hope for a united church that can face the world. There are lots of things Christians of any denomination can do, but the ecumenical aim of an organisational united church doesn't seem to be happening. When they try to hammer out statements of belief, they cannot agree on the core of the Gospel...Paul is clear in this passage that there is only one Gospel, and perhaps the church is losing ground so much because we have 'diluted the standard solution' as I was saying earlier.   Supposing you went into a pharmacy and the dispensing chemist asked what you wanted. You could say 'Well, I saw my next door neighbour taking some nice pink pills, and I wondered whether you could give me some. I'm not feeling too well.' The chemist might think you were crazy. He would certainly would want to know what your medical problem was and whether you'd seen your doctor. He would point out that your neighbour's nice pink pills might not be helpful in tackling what is wrong with you.

Only this week we've been hearing in the news that the medical authorities are going to target heart disease by prescribing one specific kind of pill. So it is with our soul's disease. It looks like it is going to be increasingly difficult for Christians to say that there is only one Gospel, one Saviour and one way of salvation, that the Lord Jesus Christ is the Way, the Truth and the Life. The Christian gospel and the Christian's Saviour are not on a level playing field with other messages and other religious leaders. The Christian message is qualitatively distinctive from other messages in its claim that Jesus has risen from the dead and that there is no other name under heaven given amongst men by which we can be saved. It seems to be more 'in your face' in Galatians chapter one because Paul in these first two chapters is defending the Christian message of sovereign grace from a **personal** standpoint. In chapters three and four he is arguing from a **doctrinal** standpoint, and in chapters five and 6 he is arguing from a **practical** standpoint. But more of that later!

QUESTIONS FOR DISCUSSION.
1 V 6-10

1. Why is Paul 'astonished' at the Galatian Christians ?

2. 'Act in haste, repent at leisure.'   Should Paul have been so outspoken so early in the letter?   (defend your conclusion)

3. How many 'gospels' are there?   How can you tell the real one?

4. Do you know of any individual or groups who 'pervert' the Gospel?

5. Are 'anathemas' 'out' today? Would you use this term for anyone?

CHAPTER 4.

THE ROOTS OF PAUL'S GOSPEL
Galatians Chapter 1 verses 11-24.

In the first 10 verses of Galatians chapter 1, Paul dispensed with the first century pleasantries of conventional letter-writing, and swung into a powerful defence of his divine calling as an apostle. His feathers had been well and truly ruffled by false teachers who rubbished his standing, and Paul also swung into a defence of his message that the Christian believers at Galatia had been born again into freedom. This freedom was based on God's free and sovereign grace, and Christ's indwelling peace, bought at great price by Christ's sacrifice for sin, which had rescued them and brought their lives into alignment with God's plan. Paul was aghast that the Galatian believers were buckling under pressure from the old guard of false teachers so soon after hearing Paul's gospel. They were behaving like turncoats, and the false teachers were troublemakers whose message was a no-no.

You might have expected Paul, having given them a good telling-off, to challenge them to give themselves to God and His grace again – but he doesn't, at least not here. Someone said that if you are threatened by frosty weather, the best thing to do is to put on a good fire! So Paul, an inspired writer, warms their hearts by repeating words about the gospel (verse 11-12) which he had used about himself in verse 1, and then going on to tell about his own experience of God before, at, and after his conversion. Sometimes when we're planning a holiday, we read the blurb about the place we're thinking of going to, but our minds can be made up when we see an inset photo of a happy family who went there, lived in that hotel, enjoyed the good food, swam in the pool, and had a great time. Personal testimony is a strong way of confirming the facts. Personal experience gives the truth legs. Perhaps we should read part of the section to illustrate what I mean. Here it is in 'The Message':

'Know this – I am most emphatic here, friends – this great

message I delivered to you is not mere human optimism. I didn't receive it through the traditions, and I wasn't taught it in some school. I got it straight from God, received the message direct from Jesus Christ.'

I'm sure you've heard the story of my earlier life when I lived in the Jewish way. In those days I went all out in persecuting God's church. I was systematically destroying it. I was so enthusiastic about the traditions of my ancestors that I advanced head and shoulders above my peers in my career. Even then God had designs on me. Why, when I was still in my mother's womb He chose and called me out of sheer generosity! Now He has intervened and revealed His Son to me so that I might joyfully tell non-Jews about Him.'

It is a great freedom which we should treasure that we live in a free country, which used to be called 'the land of the Book.' Which book? You may be asking. When one of our greatest writers, Sir Walter Scott, was dying, he said to his friend Lockhart 'bring down the book' Lockhart asked this very question, because Scott's library was lined with books. 'There is only one Book,' said Scott, 'the Bible.'

Back to the Bible, and Galatians 1 verses 11-24. In verses 11 and 12, Paul emphasises his claim that there was nothing second-hand about his Christian experience. He got his message directly from Jesus Christ, first-hand.

Before his conversion, Saul the Pharisee/Paul the apostle was a three-way fanatic! We don't use the word 'fanatic' very much. We use an abbreviated form when we talk about a football 'fan'. In the days of colour-coated tram routes, the 'green tram' went from Glasgow to Airdrie, and some Rangers supporters used to walk to Airdrie when their team were playing there, rather than travel on a green tram. They would have called themselves 'real fans'. Green was the colour worn by their arch-rivals, Glasgow Celtic.

As I said, Paul was a real fan in three different ways:
First of all, he was a fanatic in harassment, 'I went all-out in persecuting God's church' he says. He rooted out and hounded the pockets of Christian believers, and gave them a hard time of it. Secondly, he was a fanatic in destruction of God's church.

Acts 8 verse 3 tells us he conducted house to house searches for believers, and in his testimony before King Agrippa, in Acts 26 verse 10, he says he actually voted for the death penalty for Christians. Why was he so bitter? Perhaps the Christian message of a Messiah who died on a Roman Cross stuck in the throat of someone who had a triumphalist view of a conquering Messiah who would clear Israel of the hated occupying power. Charles Cousar says: 'One reason why Paul had reacted so vigorously as he did in opposition to the first Christians was their incomprehensible message about a crucified Messiah.'... How could they preach that a Person admittedly cursed by the Law as seen in the manner of his death, had been raised by God from the dead?' Thirdly, he was a fanatic about Jewish tradition, and became an expert exponent of it, outstripping his contemporaries. He knew the Jewish Bible, that is the Christian Old Testament, inside-out and back to front, in Hebrew, the original language it was written in, and also in Greek, in the Septuagint version. He also knew what every rabbi worth his salt had said about the Jewish Law, for centuries back.

It's difficult to knock a fanatic off his perch, especially a well-enamelled, laminated one like Paul. In fact only God could, and did, dislodge him from his position! In retrospect, Paul gives God the glory that God had been working in his life ever since he was a foetus, and as a new-born baby fresh 'from my mother's womb'! Paul would have said a thumping 'Amen' to the Psalm of David number 139 'Lord you have searched me and you know me....you hem me in - behind and before; you have laid your hand upon me....where can I go from your Spirit? Where can I flee from your presence? If I go up to the heavens, you are there; if I make my bed in the depths, you are there...for you created my inmost being; you knit me together in my mother's womb ...your eyes saw my unformed body. All the days ordained for me were written in your book before one of them came to be.' My sermon points on this psalm are valid for all of us. I wonder whether you have ever thought like this: God knows everything about us...God is everywhere around us...God made everything within us...'

Chapter 1 verses 15 and 16 are marked by a sea-change in the Subject of the sentence. Most of us have too much ego in our cosmos. The previous verses are full of capital 'I' and egotistical 'my'. Now God becomes the subject of the sentence, the new Person at the heart of Paul's life. God had created him, God's mercy had found him, and God's grace had called him. Walter Hansen has an interesting statement on this section: 'The contrast between Paul and the Galatian believers stands out in bold relief here. As a Jew, he had turned from his preoccupation with the distinctive Jewish way of life to serve the risen Christ; as Gentiles, they were turning from their focus on Christ to a preoccupation with a Jewish way of life. No wonder Paul calls them 'foolish Galatians' in chapter 3 verse 1.

Before his conversion, Paul was the implacable enemy of the Christians and their gospel. Sometimes we wonder why some people are so antagonistic to Christians, the church and the Bible. Admittedly, some Christians are too much 'in your face', and what they think is the offence of the Cross is really the offensiveness of the Christians. We also have to admit that there are false and phoney Christians, even false and phoney ministers, who are in the church for what they can get out of it, and would be useless in any other job. But we shouldn't give up using money because there is counterfeit about. The existence of counterfeit tells us that the real thing must be worth copying! And the Lord knows the phoneys, just as the bank recognises counterfeit...A lot of the antagonism to Christians can be traced to our sinful nature, and its antagonism to God. Furthermore, a lot of people reject the Bible because they resent its authority, and reject the views of people they label 'fundamentalists' because they take the Bible's claims about itself seriously. It is very difficult to explain the apparent discrepancies of the Bible. My Bible class teacher, who was a naval architect, had huge problems about the Bible before his conversion, particularly about the miracle stories of the Old Testament. He told us that he came to discover that his biggest problem was not his intellectual difficulties about the Bible, but the problem of his sin before God. He said when he had the sin question dealt with through repenting and believing in Christ for salvation, a lot of his other difficulties fell into place. Mark Twain said it was not the bits of the Bible he didn't understand that scared him, it was the bits he did understand!

In verse 16, Paul provides a beautiful description of his own life, and the Christian life generally. The New International Version translates: 'God...was pleased to reveal His Son in me, that I might preach Him among the Gentiles.' No longer did Paul need to worry about mental mastery of rules and regulations. He had encountered the risen Christ, and God's sweet invasion of the Holy Spirit's presence had brought him into an intimate relationship with The Lord Jesus. The dark curtain of his bitterness and cruelty had been removed, and the light of Christ could shine out from him. Prenatal choice had been followed by historical call and personal revelation. Later this brilliant young Pharisee was to be set loose by God among the Gentiles, who would read his life like a book sent from God, rather like people read Christians today. The famous Baptist preacher CH Spurgeon said Gad wants sermons in boots, rather than sermons in books (the Victorians tended to wear boots rather than shoes):

'Not only in the words you speak, not only by your deeds confessed,
But in the most unconscious way is Christ expressed.
Is a beatific smile? a holy light upon your brow?
Oh No! I felt His presence when you laughed just now.
For me, 'twas not the truth you taught,
To you so clear, to me so dim,
But when you came yourself
You brought a sense of Him.
And from your eyes He beckons me,
And from your heart His love is shed,
'Till I lose sight of you, and see the Christ instead.'

In terms of priorities as a Christian preacher, stage one for Paul was the revelation of the risen Christ. Paul would agree with the view of the hymn-writer who said:
'Since my eyes were fixed on Jesus I've lost sight of all beside,
So enchained my spirit's vision gazing at the crucified.'

The development of that vision resulted in a powerful and

optimistic presentation of Good News to the Gentiles., or non-Jews. This was to take up Paul's life, although his usual pattern in any town was to begin at the synagogue if there was one, and if he was shown the door, or flung out of it, to go into the street or hire a hall to spread his message.

Now we have to examine Paul's explanations why he did not 'go to school' with the Jerusalem experts.

We're looking at chapter 1 verses 11-24, and especially in this section chapter 1 verses 16 and 17. Some people are corrosively critical! Not content with rubbishing his standing and undermining his teaching, the false teachers said he was able to share what he knew because he had copied it from the apostles of Jesus who lived in Jerusalem! This was a colossal cheek! In the remaining section of chapter 1, Paul gives three 'notes for absence' from attending the Jerusalem 'school.'

Those of us who have been schoolteachers are familiar with pupils' excuses and notes for absence. For example : ' Please excuse Jimmy being absent as his nose was running through a hole in his shoe', or 'please excuse Jean being absent as she vomited up the whole of Argyle Street', or 'Please excuse Peter being off as he had dior (scored out), diar (scored out) 'a sore head'.

Well, in this passage, Paul gives his three notes for absence, proving he did not 'go to school' on the apostles at Jerusalem. He writes : 'I did not consult any man, nor did I go up to Jerusalem to see those who were apostles before me...'

NOTE FOR ABSENCE NUMBER 1. I couldn't be indoctrinated by the 'Jerusalem set' because I was in Arabia. The events of the following 18 verses seem to be in careful sequence, conversion - Damascus - Arabia - Damascus - Jerusalem, punctuated by the recurrent word 'then'. The three years in Arabia (probably the Nabataean desert) could date from his conversion. The Acts information seems compressed and the visit to Jerusalem might have been made from Antioch. These years in Arabia were vital. They paralleled the three years the disciples spent with Jesus, and bear comparison with time taken nowadays for an alcoholic or drug addict to totally 'dry out'. Paul's highly-trained mind would have to go over years of indoctrination, and his whole theological position revamped. These were hidden years of quietness, vital for listening to God, and having that massive brain of his re-orientated. Walter Hansen has an interesting comment on the hidden years: 'In our days, when celebrities are converted, the religious media rush to publicise their conversions for the widest possible audience. Put them on TV; feature them in prime-time talk shows. But this immediate publicity can be dangerous for the spiritual health of new converts. Under the harsh, glaring lights of the media they have no space to think through the implications of their new faith, to work through their inconsistencies and to listen to the Lord. They sometimes feel used and abused. They need time, as we all do, to be hidden from the public eye in order to grow and deepen in their faith. Hidden years seem to be part of God's plan for His servants. Moses spent forty years in the desert before his day in Pharaoh's court. Jesus spent about eighteen years working in the carpenter's shop in Nazareth. Paul writes about a would-be Christian leader in 1 Timothy 3 ; 'He must not be a new believer, lest the position go to his head, and the devil trip him up.'

I became a Christian and was trained in what was then known as Lambill Mission and is now known as Lambhill Evangelical Church. The Sunday preachers there were mainly ordinary working people with an extraordinary experience of God and the Bible. Most of them had rudimentary education; one of them said he had been through Glasgow University – in his horse and cart! But most of them had been to what they called 'The Holy Ghost Bible School.' Despite having to work hard, they had carved out times of quiet when they could study the Bible and listen to God, like Paul in Arabia. 'Take from our souls the strain and stress, and let our ordered lives confess the beauty of Thy peace.'

Paul produces his **'NOTE FOR ABSENCE NUMBER 2'** in verses 18-20, by pointing out that he visited Jerusalem later (three years), and briefly, (two weeks, to get acquainted) and only saw two of the apostles (Peter and James). This visit probably followed his unceremonious escape from Damascus, down the city walls in a basket! (Acts 9 v 26). The Jerusalem visit was nothing as major as the false teachers were suggesting. No doubt Paul would be interested in Peter's account of Jesus' life and ministry, Peter would be interested in Paul's life story and adventures, and they would seek to build a good working relationship for their future work for God in the churches. The account of the Jerusalem Council in Acts 15 illustrates James' position of leadership of the Jerusalem Church. In Galatians 1 verse 20, Paul confirms the complete reliability of his account : 'I'm telling you the absolute truth in this'.

The Jerusalem visit was no doubt also a sight-seeing trip, although Paul was familiar with the sights and sounds of the city, having studied there under Rabbi Gamaliel. There was no way Paul could have a full course on the comprehensive nature of the Gospel in two weeks! There was also no way Peter could pass on to Paul his apostolic commission. Yet Paul was there not only to establish bonds of fellowship, but to listen to Peter as what Professor FF Bruce called 'the primary informant on matters it was now important that Paul should know – the details of Jesus' ministry and the 'tradition' of teaching which derived from Him.'

Paul's **NOTE FOR ABSENCE NUMBER 3** is given in chapter 1 verses 21-24. He did not have the opportunity to 'go to school' on the Jerusalem apostles because his ministry had begun in the regions of Syria and Cilicia. He and Barnabas were commissioned at the church in Syrian Antioch by the Holy Spirit and the church for the Gentile mission. We can read all about it in Acts chapter 13 'One day as they were worshipping God – they were also fasting as they waited for guidance- the Holy Spirit spoke: 'Take Barnabas and Saul and commission them for the work I have called them to do. So they commissioned them. In that circle of intensity and obedience, of fasting and praying, they laid hands on their head and sent them off.'

Galatians 2 verse one gives a time reference of fourteen years after that first visit, or possibly after his conversion, so it is clear that Paul is clearing himself of any charges that his gospel is a second-hand rehash of stuff he was taught by the Jerusalem apostles.

Our discussion raises the whole question of whom you can believe nowadays. How about the car salesman? In the 1960s my neighbour was looking for a second-hand car, and pointed out the tell-tale bubbles in the paintwork of a car. The salesman called over a mechanic, who said there was no rust there, punched the wing of the car, and put his fist through it! Needless to say, there was no sale...Or how about the politicians? Someone said of a politician when Harold Wilson was Prime Minister that if you plugged him into a lie detector, he would fuse the National Grid? Or how about these people who come round the door from the cults? A gentleman tried to argue about the Greek text of John 1 verse 1 with my philosophy tutor, who was out working with his gardening clothes on.. The visitor was arguing that the Greek text of John 1 verse 1 should be translated 'the Word was a god, rather than the word was God.' My tutor asked him what the Greek word for 'a' was, (there isn't a Greek word for 'a'), and sent him packing for pretending to know Greek...

Can you trust what the Bible says? Bertrand Russell was arguably the greatest philosopher of the twentieth century, who wrote a book 'Why I am not a Christian', and yet he could only make two minor criticisms of the character of Christ as revealed in the Gospels. Could you join me in accepting what the Bible says about its human authors in the second letter of Peter ?: 'Men they were, but driven along by the Holy Spirit, they wrote the words of God.'

Paul's wide-ranging explanation, and the three notes for absence, brings us back to the twin towers which characterise Galatians chapter one. Paul's standing and calling and apostleship have a divine origin, and so does his Gospel. He did not get it for services rendered. He was the hated enemy of believers, with flimsy connections with the apostolic band in Jerusalem. Jock Troup, the revivalist evangelist of the twenties in East Anglia and the North East of Scotland, was asked in scathing tones by a journalist 'where do these revivals come from, anyway?' Jock grabbed the journalist's lapels in his huge paws and forced him to his knees. He then released his right hand and pointed heavenwards 'They come from GOD'. (the journalist scurried away with great relief !). Paul would have produced the same argument about his apostleship and his Gospel. Paul's Gospel cannot be at variance with the Gospel of Christ if he got it from Christ. Nor is Paul's Gospel a church production if Paul had flimsy connections with the church leaders. He got the message directly from Christ. John Stott writes: 'If Paul was right in asserting that his Gospel was not man's but God's, then to reject Paul is to reject God.' You sure done slobbered a bibful there, brother John.

However, as you may guess, the false teachers kept snapping at his heels like a pack of Jack Russells, and if they could not divide Paul's Gospel from the Lord or the church, how about trying to drive a wedge between the message of Paul and the message of Peter? If you can find time to read on into the next chapter, we'll go into message and relationships in Galatians chapter 2.

QUESTIONS FOR DISCUSSION.
1 V 11-24.

1. From 1 v 11-12. What is distinctive about the Gospel from these verses?

2. What was so alarming about Paul's profile (verses 13-14)? Is there anything alarming about yours?

3. How can we trace God's influence on our childhood? (1 v 15)

4. Why would Paul withdraw to Arabia so soon after his conversion ? Is it good to have times of spiritual retreat?

5. Share some instances of people whose lives have led others to Praise God (see 1 v 24).

OUTLINE OF GALATIANS
CHAPTER TWO.

Fourteen years later, responding to God's leading, Paul visited Jerusalem with Barnabas and Titus. He shared the content of his Gospel privately with church leaders. They never insisted that Titus should be circumcised, despite the pressurising activities of false 'brothers' who had infiltrated the group. Paul was inflexible with them, and his message was acceptable to the Christians there, who validated his work of preaching the Gospel to Gentiles. This counter-balanced Peter's work with Jews. God confirmed the work done by Peter and Paul, and James, Peter and John welcomed Paul and endorsed his message and ministry, asking only that Paul and his friends continued to give to the poor, which was already their intention and practice.

Paul had to confront Peter at Antioch for his inconsistency in separating himself from eating with Gentiles, after the pro-circumcision party arrived. Paul pointed out the divisive implications of Peter's action for the Christian Church, highlighting the difference between being put right with God through trusting Christ, rather than keeping the law. Peter's action looked like coercing the Gentiles to turn into Jews! Our sinful practices undermine our justified state, so that we break God's law. Being a Christian involves self-death, and a new life energised by the indwelling Christ, whose love and self-giving did not wipe out the grace of God, nor did it make Christ's death valueless.

CHAPTER 5.

TITUS, A TEST CASE FOR THE GOSPEL.
Galatians Chapter 2 verses 1- 10

This section of the letter brings us to look at Paul and his relationships. It seems he could never escape the false teachers. They had been chasing him almost as soon as he had been to Galatia, and some of the locals had accepted his message of God's free and sovereign grace. They were like dogs snapping at his heels. I remember a visit I made to the great city of Sao Paulo in Brazil, and the mangy street dogs who used to follow me on my morning trips to test out my Portuguese for two cartons of milk and six rolls. Even changing my route to the wee shop couldn't shake them off. I carried an aluminium clothes pole in case they attacked me, and I was particularly concerned about one hairy tyke. Paul seemed to be similarly unable to shake off the false teachers who were on his case. 'He's not a real apostle,' they said. He tried to answer that by asserting God's divine call to his task. 'His Gospel is inadequate' they said – it surely isn't enough simply to believe in the Lord Jesus Christ, and enter into peace and grace, a sense of deliverance and a gratitude for Christ's rescue. Surely this 'born free' message must include circumcision and Jewish observance. Paul reiterated that his Gospel was not only enough, but it was the only Gospel. Anything else was a travesty, and those who preached any other message were under the strongest condemnation. Then they followed him down another street: 'He got his message second-hand from the Jerusalem apostles. He's just a dummy for the Jerusalem ventriloquists.' Paul responded by telling how he went away for three years to learn from God in the quietness how to redirect his encyclopaedic knowledge of the Old Testament into the service of Jesus. When he did visit Jerusalem, the visit was delayed (3 years after his conversion), brief (2 weeks) and limited (he only met 2 apostles). The visit helped establish fellowship links with Peter and James. So then, like the pariahs of Sao Paulo dogging my footsteps, they went down another street: 'Paul is a loner. He doesn't have anything to do with the Jerusalem version of the Gospel and he operates independently of Peter and the Jerusalem church leaders.' Of course, they had to say that, if they were appealing to Jerusalem church practice to influence the Galatian believers into a Jewish lifestyle.

Let's hear a bit of the text, using the Message paraphrase: 'Fourteen years after that first visit, Barnabas and I went up to Jerusalem and took Titus with us. I went to clarify with them what had been revealed to me. At that time I placed before them exactly what I was preaching to the non-Jews. I did this in private with the leaders, those held in esteem by the church, so that our concern would not become a controversial public issue, marred by ethnic tensions, exposing my years of work to public denigration and endangering my present ministry. Significantly, Titus, non-Jewish though he was, was not required to be circumcised. While we were in conference, we were infiltrated by spies pretending to be Christians, who slipped in to find out just how free true Christians are. Their ulterior motive was to reduce us to their brand of slavery. We didn't give them the time of day. We were determined to preserve the truth of the Message for you.'

The chapter raises a whole range of issues on relationships, which we'll hope to explore here and now.

In chapter 2, Paul shows that he is nobody's messenger boy. The Galatians should have accepted his Gospel as from God, and should have maintained total loyalty to it. In chapter 2 Paul balances the personal nature of his Gospel with the fact that he did not preach it without the approval and support of the original apostles, and the Jerusalem church. He showed a fine balance between deference and determination.

How do you get on with other people? Do you relate well? Some of us are quiet but happy family members or work-mates who get on well with our fellow human beings. Others of us are in-your-face, confrontational and loud people. Sometimes we assign character traits to the areas we come from, and use demeaning terms to describe others. In Scotland some of the Highland people are suspicious of Islanders, and use phrases like 'A Skye man is a fly man'. Or Aberdonians or Paisley buddies or Fifers are mean. Or Glaswegians are drunken. We even make up jokes about them... For example, an Aberdonian asked the grave-diggers at his father's funeral whether they took a drink, and when they said they did, he said 'well, look at that coffin, and let that be a lesson to you.' Or the Paisley man whose only response to seeing Niagara Falls was 'whit a waste o' watter!'. Or the Fifer who told his children that the gas meter was a savings bank...Or the Glasgow man at Hogmanay in a Bud Neill cartoon, who confused the bus driver by saying 'Take me drunk, A'm home!'

In the modern world it seems easier to live in isolation from others, but realistically, we are gregarious creatures, and we bounce off each other daily like the pebbles on the beach, and sometimes knock the rough edges off one another. Someone said that Tarzan of the Apes is an impossible fiction, and in Daniel Defoe's book 'Robinson Crusoe' we sense the plaintive loneliness of Crusoe before he meets up with Man Friday.

Bad relationships split up families. On a BBC news programme recently, they were discussing the murder of three teenagers in London over the last few days. One speaker said one of the main reason for violence was lack of education in how to control our emotions, that the absence of a Dad in many families deprived the youngsters of a good male role model, and that the Government should be making mum and dads stay together...It was all a question of relationships.

 Bad relationships also split up churches. It can be about what colour to decorate the church hall, or how many rings there would be in the cooker on the church kitchen, but more often that not the cause is a controlling, manipulative, powerful individual or group flexing their psychological muscle. Walter Hansen writes: 'Disruptive mystics and lone rangers have often split and splintered the church. People with exceptional gifts and strengths are sometimes prone to exercise their gifts in divisive ways.' Someone has said that division is the curse of Christianity. Disruption in churches makes it difficult to assess whether church growth is happening, or is what we think is church growth actually transfer growth, with believers simply transferring allegiance to some more appealing group. They used to say that there were two kinds of growth in Baptist churches – extension churches and ex-tension churches...Elsewhere in this letter, we'll see Paul arguing for unity, and we'll see how he met a difficult relationship problem head-on, and how with God's help, he found a good solution to the problem.

There was an interesting juxta-position of personalities and backgrounds here. Paul brought a team along to the Council of Jerusalem – he came with Barnabas and Titus. Barnabas was a highly-respected Jewish Christian and Titus was an uncircumcised Gentile Christian (2 v 3). Barnabas' given name was Joseph, but his nickname meant 'son of encouragement'. People like him are worth their weight in gold in any group. Christian or non-Christian. He was a welcoming, outgoing man of grace, helpful and generous. He did not have a 'give-even, get-even' mentality like so many people.

During the days of the Berlin Wall, pre-1989, the East Berliners decided to send their West Berlin adversaries a little 'gift'. They loaded a dump truck with rubbish, broken bricks, building materials, and anything else with zero value. They drove the truck across the border, got clearance, and dumped it on the West Berlin side. Many West Berliners wanted to get even, but a wise man's counsel triumphed and they responded by loading a dump truck with food, clothing, medical supplies and a host of essential items. They carefully unloaded it on the East Berlin side and left a neat sign that read 'each gives according to his ability'. Barnabas was the kind of man who would repay evil with good. He deserved his nickname 'son of encouragement'. When Paul was excluded from the Jerusalem Church after his conversion, it was Barnabas who took Paul, brought him to the Jerusalem apostles, and spoke up for him. Later, when the Jerusalem church sent Barnabas to Antioch to supervise the mission to the Gentiles, his heart was large enough to accept the new practice of including Gentiles. He chose Paul to join him in ministering to the Antioch church. Paul could not have picked a better man than Barnabas for his team at the Jerusalem Council.

As we said earlier, Titus was a Greek Christian who had not been circumcised. Some people would say that Paul was creating difficulties here, that bringing Titus was an inflammatory act of provocation. The false teachers, the Judaisers who infiltrated the meeting, were furious. The issue was not circumcision; the issue was Christian freedom or Jewish bondage. Titus was the embodiment of Paul's Gospel, included in the team to illustrate Paul's conviction that Greek Christians were 'born free', glad to experience the grace of God without becoming Jews to be accepted into the Church of Jesus Christ. Walter Hansen says: 'The best place to start building unity in the church is to start working with a team of diverse people who are united by their common faith in Christ and their mission....it offers the opportunity to show the unifying power of the Gospel.' Paul stood firm in the presence of the apostles and against the Judaisers, who put pressure on to have Titus circumcised, and the apostles did not require this of Titus. This was a test case for free grace.

We have been following the interaction between Paul and his chosen team of Barnabas 'the son of encouragement' (a Hebraism meaning 'encouraging fellow'), a highly respected Jewish Christian leader, and Titus, an uncircumcised Greek Christian, the 'false brothers' who infiltrated the Jerusalem meeting, and the apostles and believers from the Jerusalem church. Paul says the infiltrators were there 'to spy on the freedom we have in Christ Jesus, and to make us slaves.'(verse 4) There were a few solid outcomes from this meeting: Titus was not compelled to be circumcised, and Paul's gospel was not added to nor embellished in any way by the Jerusalem leaders. The spheres of ministry – Paul and Barnabas to non-Jews and Peter and the Jerusalem leaders – were formally defined. Paul and his friends were encouraged to show a caring attitude in treating the poor, which they were keen to do anyway.
Only one problem remained – Peter's eating habits ! John Stott calls this incident 'One of the most tense and dramatic episodes in the New Testament.' Peter had been eating regularly with the non-Jews until the conservative group arrived from Jerusalem. From then on he separated from the non-Jews, and ate with the conservative Jewish clique. 'even Barnabas was swept along in the charade' (verse 13), and seemed to become one of the Jewish 'cronies.'
Paul tackled Peter head-on on this issue, and charged Peter with

being a turn-coat. To the Jerusalem lot, anyone who ate pork, broke the food laws, and became a sinner. (the rule of thumb for the Jews was that the animals they were allowed to eat had to BOTH chew the cud and divide the hoof.) To Paul, this was a matter of grace. Apart from producing a church with two clearly-divided classes, behaviour like this brought the Gospel of free grace into disrepute – acceptance by God was not by performance-rated eating and drinking , but by total trusting.

Anyone interested in group dynamics would be interested in this section of Galatians. It is a triangular situation. **Firstly,** there is the man of God, Paul, flanked by two men who are recent converts, and a total study in contrasts – Titus, probably a young Greek destined for responsibility in the church later, and Barnabas the outgoing Jewish man of integrity. **Secondly,** there is the group of Jerusalem apostles headed by Peter and James. They are honestly trying to direct things in a way pleasing to the Lord, and good for the unity of the church, within the parameters of their very conservative outlook. The topic in tension is the theme topic of these studies : are Christians really 'born free'? Or are there hurdles to clear apart from repentance and faith in the Lord Jesus Christ? **Thirdly,** there is the group of Judaising infiltrators who arrive in Jerusalem with their own agenda, intent on gate-crashing the party, and forcing issues in their direction, so that new Christians would have Jewish requirements imposed on them. How did it all work out the way it did? – cliff-hanger!... We'll hope to find out....

The Bible is a wonderful book. Paul says in his 2nd letter to Timothy that all Scripture is 'God-breathed', either expiration, that is breathed out by God (I always remember the speech balloons in the comics I read as a child), or inspiration, breathed into by God, like the Adam story in Genesis 2 'God breathed into his nostrils the breath of life, and man became a living soul.' Of all the 66 books in this divine library, Galatians is a gripper, and the section we are dealing with has so many lessons to teach us:

How should we behave when we meet people with whom we disagree, or with people we don't like?

The old advice is good – count to ten! Which means don't

speak or act impulsively. As a Christian, I have found that your treatment of someone, or your behaviour towards them changes if you have prayed for them. Jesus encouraged us to pray for our enemies. We could add opponents, or even fellow-Christians! Another point is the one made by Winston Churchill, that jaw-jaw is better than Waw Waw – better to talk than to fight, or quarrel. A lot of smouldering resentment would evaporate if we just talked things over with our imagined opponent. We might even discover that our 'opponent' is really our ally...

Another good thing to do is always to be polite. We shouldn't be rude. Paul had respect for the church leaders at Jerusalem, even when he disagreed with them. They were his elders in the faith, but he learned early in his Christian life that you measure the men by the message, not vice versa. This does not mean that he altered his principles to accommodate them. He was polite but determined. I love the old-fashioned language of the seventeenth century. Oliver Cromwell once wrote to someone: ' I beseech you in the bowels of Christ, to consider whether you might be wrong in this matter...'

When I was pastoring a Baptist Church, one of our church leaders rebuked me for having fellowship with Christians outwith our church. I told him that I agreed with George Whitefield that anyone who said he loved Jesus was his brother in the Lord, and I would not move a millimetre on that.

Another thing is we should not be scared of people because of their status or reputation, if we think they are wrong. There is a time when it is right to withstand people. There is also a time when it is not right to let bullies have their way. In this passage, both Peter and Barnabas were cowed into a corner. It was not that they had abandoned their principles. They acted in this way because they were afraid of the conservative Jewish clique. I have been present on committees where I have seen people who should have known better allowing themselves to be eye-balled into submission by a few bullies or silenced by people they knew were telling lies. Paul was not being a bully here. Listen to what John Stott says on this issue: 'Was it because Paul ...couldn't control his temper or his tongue? Was he an exhibitionist who enjoyed an argument? Did he regard Peter as a dangerous rival, and leapt at an opportunity to down him?

No. None of these base passions motivated Paul...Paul acted as he did out of a deep concern for the very principle that Peter lacked. By his behaviour, Peter had compromised the essential truth of the Gospel. That truth was that guilty sinners can know God's pardon and acceptance, not by any merits of our own. Paul was willing to die defending that principle.'

A rather healthy feature of this chapter is that it shows that Christians are fallible like everyone else. Christians are imperfect people in a perfection-ridden context. Paul and Peter were Christian men called by God to special leadership tasks. They had both been very effective workers for God. Yet here is Paul opposing Peter to his face, contradicting him, and rebuking him. You can detect the sting in Paul's words in verse 14: 'If you, a Jew, live like non-Jew when you're not being observed by the watchdogs from Jerusalem, what right have you to require non-Jews to conform to Jewish customs?'
We must face the fact that we live in a world full of conflict, although we are twenty centuries later than this chapter. The battlegrounds are different, but the principles are the same. The gospel is the good news of sinful men being brought into a new freedom by being justified freely by God's grace. Our duty is first of all to live in a way that matches the gospel. Peter in Acts 10 had a vision from God about the clean and the unclean. He also accepted the Gospel, but in this incident he did not behave in an appropriate way for someone who had been born free. Secondly, there are times when we must stand our ground against those who deny the gospel, and challenge them, and refuse to be bullied into submission to their viewpoint. We have to be like Martin Luther who stated his position and then said: 'Here I stand, God helping me.'

Another tremendous truth which emerges from a study of this section dealing with Titus the Test Case is the honesty of the Bible. You are in the safe hands of God when you take up this Book and go on an honest search for God. You meet honesty here, because the Bible is not afraid to show that its greatest men are flawed. Israel's greatest king David was guilty of the most serious sins. Moses was occasionally an exhibitionist leader.

Isaac as an old man settled for venison cooked the way he liked it; he was the victim of his appetites in his old age. The other thing is that we can come to God as flawed people, stand before that Cross, and know that the Lord Jesus Christ can forgive us. We cannot and must not attempt to do what some of the victims of addiction do. They say, 'I'll come to church, or I'll come to God **when I've sorted myself out'** ; come as you are, today. Join the rest of us, wounded healers/wounded soldiers who will not quit the fight because we must follow our Great Saviour and Commander. Cry out to God where you are, and as you are. Joseph Hart's old hymn says 'If you tarry till you're better, you will never come at all.'

QUESTIONS FOR DISCUSSION
2 V 1 - 10

1. Was Paul being controversial and provocative by taking Titus with him, or were there other reasons? If so, what were they?

2. How did the Jerusalem leaders react to Titus?

3. What kind of people infiltrate churches in order to cause trouble? (2 v 4-5)

4. What conclusions did the Jerusalem leaders come to about Paul's Ministry? What area of ministry was common to Paul and them?

CHAPTER 6.

PERSONALITY CLASH
Galatians Chapter 2 verses 11-21.

The first two chapters contain a personal defence of Paul's status as an apostle, his message of God's free and sovereign grace, through which He forgives sinners solely through unadorned faith in the sacrifice Christ made for our sins, to rescue us and set us free from the bondage which had us in its grip. He waxed hot and strong against any so-called 'alternative gospel', claiming that his message stood supreme and alone. In the early part of chapter two, he tells how he brought Titus, an uncircumcised Greek Christian to Jerusalem, and how the Jerusalem Council did not bear down with any requirements like keeping Jewish food laws and ceremonies nor insisting that Titus should be circumcised. When Peter and Barnabas buckled under the pressure of the false teachers who dogged Paul's footsteps, and left off having table fellowship with Gentiles, Paul faced Peter up with the inconsistency of his position. How could Christians preach the freedom of grace, and then fall into the bondage of performance as a way of pleasing God? That is why this section reveals a personality clash.

William Barclay sets it out very clearly: Paul's argument runs like this. He said to Peter 'You shared the table with the Gentiles. You ate and lived as they did; therefore you approved in principle that there is one way for Jew and Gentile alike. How can you reverse your whole decision? You were quite willing to live like a Gentile; and now you have swung round, and you want the Gentiles to be circumcised and take the law upon them and become Jews.' John Stott said 'In resisting Peter, Paul preserved both the truth of the Gospel, and the international brotherhood of the church.'

Walter Hansen points out that the social crisis in the Antioch church was exactly the same as the crisis faced by the churches in Galatia: Gentiles were being forced to live like Jews in order to be acceptable by Jews. The social crisis masked a fundamental theological issue: Is law-keeping or gospel-believing the basis for determining fellowship between Jewsh ad Gentile Christians? It's a twenty-first century issue as well as a first century issue. If there is a God and I want to get to know Him, have I to work my socks off to please him, by keeping the Ten Commandments, and as well as the moral law, have I also to keep the ceremonial law – be circumcised, join the Jewish community and study and fast and pray and give alms? This was the stance of the Jew and the Judaising false teacher. Today it would be : do I have to fulfil a set of performance-related criteria, like attending church, being kind to granny and the cat, wearing a cross or a crucifix round my neck, giving regularly to charities, being a friend of the earth, living an upright life, embodying in my life-style a set of negatives, like no smoking/drinking/gambling/fornicating, so that God will be pleased with me, and give me a pat on the head? Or can it all be summed up in a phrase: 'trust in Jesus Christ.' Can it be as simple as that

Here is the Message translation of what Paul wrote in Chapter 2 verses 15 and 16 : 'We Jews know that we have no advantage of birth over 'non-Jewish sinners'. We know very well that we are not set right with God by rule-keeping, but only through personal faith in Jesus Christ. How do we know? We tried it – and we had the best system of rules the world has ever seen! Convinced that no human being can please God by self-improvement, we believed in Jesus Christ as the Messiah so that we might be set right before God by trusting in the Messiah, not by trying to be good...'

This section of Galatians takes us to the beating heart of the Gospel, which is how to be 'set right with God', as our reading put it. It surely could not be right that the Jews should come to God by law, and the Gentiles should come to God by grace. That is why Paul assumes the position of the Jew and the Judaiser at the beginning of verse15. Jesus did not tell us to win salvation through the kind of butcher-meat we ate, but by throwing ourselves unreservedly on the grace of God. I could probably picture it best in two connections – the market-place and the law-court. We begin with the Old Testament imagery of righteousness. As you know, the Old Testament was written originally in Hebrew. Nearly all Hebrew nouns are derived from verbs, and the Hebrew verb from which the word 'righteousness' is derived means 'to conform to a norm or standard or template, or rule.' So in Old Testament thought, you can have a righteous or just fig, or righteous weights and measures, and outwith Biblical terms, you could have a righteous camel. This means that this fig, or this ephah (a unit of weight) or this camel, would conform to all the standards you expect from them – for example four-leggedness, a certain shape of its head, a hump (or two!), and so on. Now that I am retired, and can meander round the supermarket with my wife Jean, I can see in the fruit and veg department of Asda that all the pears are 'unrighteous', that is none of them seem to conform to the pear-shaped norm I have in my head for a pear! When we move these ideas into the realm of the character of God, we are all unrighteous, none of us matches the divine standards for purity, holiness, justice, and so on.

Our generation generally refuses to recognise the abysmal depths of evil in the human heart, and refuses to realise that Public Enemy Number One is neither ignorance (although 7 million people in Britain cannot read), nor stupidity, nor a defective social environment, but SIN, which JS Whale says 'is at the dark mysterious root of all these evils.' Whale says we don't take a sufficiently tragic view of human nature, and we cling to the forlorn hope of our inevitable progress as a species. People tell us not to take things too seriously, because we'll get better. Some wag suggested about the adolescence of the Quaker George Fox 'he had sown his wild oats, but they were only Quaker Oats.' That is, he grew out of his difficulties, and the human race will do the same. The Bible says none of us is righteous, no not one.

Let us suppose you are in prison, and are offered your freedom on condition you pay a heavy fine. The promise is real – so long as you can meet the precondition, the promise will be fulfilled. Martin Luther, the great Reformer came to share the view of Augustine that we just don't have the resources stored away anywhere to meet the precondition. Augustine and Luther developed their theology on the basis that as you don't have the money, the promise of freedom has little relevance to your situation. We find ourselves trapped in a cell for recidivist sinners. We are like recidivist criminals, who keep on committing the same crimes, and keep on re-offending. What can we do about it?

We are like prisoners who cannot pay the heavy fine which would buy our release. The Christian Gospel has a lengthy pedigree, centuries old. It is not a flash in the pan, quick fix, which goes out of fashion. Sometime during the year 1515, (yes, that's right, as long ago as that), Martin Luther told how although he lived a blameless life as a monk, he felt he was an uneasy sinner who hated the phrase 'the righteousness of God', and he says with complete frankness, he hated the righteous God who punished sinners. He agonised towards the understanding that the righteousness of God was a passive righteousness, by which a merciful God pardons sinners, and justifies us by faith. He writes: This made me feel as though I had been born again, and as though I had entered through open gates into paradise itself. From that moment I saw the whole face of Scripture in a new light...' So both Augustine and Luther, the good news of the Gospel is that we, penniless beggars in rags that we are, have been given the necessary money to buy our freedom. The pre-condition for freedom has been met by Someone else, the Lord Jesus Christ. Alister McGrath says: ' So the God of the Christian Gospel is not a harsh Judge who rewards individuals according to their merit, but a merciful and gracious God who bestows righteousness upon sinners as a gift.' An old hymn says,

'Jesus paid it all, all to Him, all to Him I owe, sin had left a crimson stain, he washed it white as snow.'

Now let's take up the second image I mentioned earlier, and move from the market-place to the law-court. The thought centres on what is forensic, and 'justification' relates to the action of a judge in acquitting criminals. We sin because we are by nature, practice and disposition, sinners. Left to our own devices, we have a built-in bias towards evil. This causes a rupture in our relationship with God, which also affects our relationship with others. As far as our standing with God is concerned, only He can change our status from guilty to not guilty. He does that through the only truly human and righteous Person who ever lived, the Lord Jesus Christ. Jesus was neither superhuman nor subhuman; He was never more than a man, but never less than God. He was what Luther calls in his great hymn Ein Feste Burg 'God's Proper Man', and He was the only human being who did not deserve to die. But He died as our sacrifice, He died as our substitute, and He bore our sins in His body to the Cross. Our faith in Christ brings us into vital union with him, and God transfers His righteousness to us and pronounces or declares us 'not guilty'. God not only pronounces us righteous, He treats us as righteous. God does not forget our wrongdoing, for forgetting is a human failing. He chooses not to remember our sins against us anymore, and this gives us a sense of freedom which puts a spring in our step, a joy in our heart, and having justified us, God begins the process of sanctifying us. We are born again by the Holy Spirit, who now takes up residence in us, and gives us desires to grow more like Jesus. Trying to keep rules and working our socks off in order to please God never works, and at any rate, even if we lived perfectly from now on, what about our past? Part of the glory of God's justifying grace is that is retrospective. Our past is all forgiven; the blood of Jesus Christ has been shed to cover past present and future living. So Paul says, in the Message paraphrase 'I quit being a 'law man' so that I could become 'Christ's man'.'

I don't know you, whoever you are, reading this book. But I am confident that what God did for Martin Luther and millions of others down the centuries, he can do for you. Jesus didn't just die for sinners without distinction. He died for you and for me as sinners in particular. He wants us to repent of our sin and trust in the power of His death for us. He wants to clear us of that guilty conscience and inner turmoil, so that we can experience His peace, forgiveness and freedom. Here's a prayer we used to teach children to say:

'Into my heart, into my heart, come into my heart, Lord Jesus, Come in today, come in to stay, come into my heart, Lord Jesus.'

God gives us freedom and forgiveness by 'righteousness transfer'. By trusting in the Lord Jesus Christ, we are pronounced 'not guilty' by God, and are set free to serve Him.

Galatians 2 verse 20 illustrates the nature of the change which

Christians experience. Let me quote it in the new International Version: 'I have been crucified with Christ, and I no longer live, but Christ lives in me. The life I live in the body, I live by faith in the Son of God, who loved me, and gave Himself for me.' The first change here is **a change of identity, which is in effect a call to self-death.** Paul says 'I have been crucified with Christ...Paul explains the change in death and resurrection terms. We should note here that the demands of Christ are greater than the demands of any club or movement. Admittedly, when I went to play badminton for and with the Smithycroft School staff team, my partner said 'show me your scars!'...he said 'I want you fighting for every shot, running till you drop, diving till you hurt, etc.'

He stopped short of asking me to die for the life of the team! Jesus wants us every day to be committed to Him in the crucifixion of our old nature, so that He can express his life through us. Notice the qualitative difference from joining a political party or a tennis club. There is a juxta-position of Christ and Me; it's a matter of Person to Person, not Person to Movement or Organisation. This creates the exciting dynamic of a daily faith relationship. Notice also there is a huge difference in the range of our commitment. This isn't choir practice or football training once a week. This covers the whole of our lives, and all of our choices – the subjects we take at school or University, the girl we marry, how we raise our children, our career choices, our leisure pursuits, how we spend our money – the lot! Then notice what I would call the internalising of benefits. This change of identity means that I am committed to change in my life so that I live to please the One who died for me, and I have a lifestyle characterised by gratitude to God for His kindness to me in Christ. And notice that this call to self-death is a long-term thing forever and ever amen. As Christ lives out His life in me, this is not a short-term tenancy agreement. The mention of crucifixion should make us wince, for there is nothing beautiful about a cross. Oh, I know we see lovely polished wood crosses inside and outside churches, a cabinet-maker's delight. When Paul wrote about a cross, he was not thinking of polished wood or filigree silver. He was thinking about an unpolished piece of wood hacked off a tree trunk, an instrument of torture, degradation and death. In our culture, people wear crosses as jewellery. To try and work out some equivalence, it would be better to be wearing a miniature hangman's noose, or electric chair as a fashion accessory, instead of a cross. The cross was a word-symbol for an utterly degrading violent death.

Of course, this explains why there are just a small percentage of our British people involved in a Biblical church lifestyle. Imagine promoting an identity change with self-death as its keynote, when the whole trend and fashion is towards self-enhancement, self-promotion, and self-improvement! No wonder John Stott said Christianity is a subversive counter-culture.

In Galatians chapter 2 verse 20 Paul says :
'I no longer live...I now live ..' We have seen that the first change which characterises the Christian life is **a Change of Identity.** The second change is a **Change of Personality.** The oscillation between 'I Live', and 'I no longer live' illustrates the paradox of Christian living. It's a study in contrasts. You might say it's a bit like golf, which is a game of contrasts and opposites. You shape up left to slice the ball right. You hit down on the ball to hit the ball up, and so on. In Christianity too, the way up is the way down. You humble yourself, and God in grace lifts you up. You die to selfishness in order to live for Christ, and so on. If the Change in Identity called for Self-Death, the Change in Personality calls for Self-Denial. This call to Self-Denial, again runs totally against the grain of current thinking about our choices, verdicts and lifestyle. We're called to this in a generation whose heroes are people like Rambo and James Bond. We're called to this so that Christ can shine through us like the sun shines through a stained glass window. In God's sight it is better to be transparent than translucent or opaque. In this way, we can exercise a good and gracious influence on those around us. Paul says in 2nd Corinthians 'we have this treasure in jars of clay.' Whatever you've got, may not be a lot, use it, use it use it for the Lord.' We are precious to the Lord, although we are weak and ordinary people. We are called to a new identity.. The God who commanded light to shine out of darkness has shone in our hearts to give the light of the knowledge of the glory of God in the face of Jesus Christ. The

focus of our living has changed so much that the only adequate way to describe it is that a change of identity has occurred, and a change of personality has taken place. There was a Christian song which said : 'It is no longer I that liveth, but Christ that liveth in me, In me In me, Jesus is alive in me, It is no longer I that liveth, but Christ that liveth in me.'

Let's try to round off on Paul's wonderful definition of Christian living in Galatians 2 verse 20 (New International Version) : 'I have been crucified with Christ and I no longer live, but Christ lives in me. The life I live in the body, I live by faith in the Son of God, who loved me and gave himself for me.' The changes which are the distinctive trade-marks of Christian living are, as we say a change of Identity, and a change of Personality. The third one is a **Change of Dependency,** which involves a call to **self-surrender.** Once again, this swims against the stream of current thought, and the emphasis and the promotion of self-sufficiency, self-love and self-advancement. To be a Christian is to recognise that we have to go out of ourselves for help, from God, and develop the life of faith and prayer. We used to do abseiling with the seventy-five boys I used to lead at Scripture Union Camps at Scoughall near North Berwick. We put the boys down an eighty-foot cliff, and I used to encourage them to lean back as near to right angles to the cliff face as they could be, and rely on the safety man, and feel confident, that whatever happened, they would not fall. The terror-stricken faces of the boys going over the top for the first time gave way to joyful exhilaration that they had conquered their fears and had enjoyed an exciting experience. After the first time, there were always plenty of volunteers for extra abseiling! Living the Christian life is a bit like that. You learn to trust the Lord Jesus, and lean on Him in faith and prayer.

You learn to look to him for guidance, and enter into the exciting experiences of dependence on Him.

Paul could never forget to thank His Lord that the Son of God 'loved me, and gave Himself for me.' It took nothing less than Christ's sacrificial death, and the experience of God's grace in the Gospel, for Paul, and me, and any of you who are reading to have this sense of freedom, this heart at peace, and this mind at ease. I pray that God will bless each one of you who are reading, and that you will enter into God's best for your life by trusting in all that the Lord Jesus has done so that you can experience these changes. Charles Wesley wrote about 6000 hymns. One of them says 'the arms of love that compass me would all mankind embrace.' That is what God is like!

QUESTIONS FOR DISCUSSION
2 v 11-21

1.   Is confrontation ever right in a loving fellowship?   What was the main issue between Paul and Peter?

2.   Are there any issues which cause, or could cause, confrontation in today's churches?

3.   Verses 15-16 mention 'justified' THREE times.   What is 'justification by faith', and why is it important?

4   Why do you think Paul means when he says: 'I have been crucified With Christ' ?

OUTLINE OF GALATIANS
CHAPTER THREE.

Paul is amazed that the Galatians have abandoned the vivid preaching of faith in Christ crucified that he thinks they have been bewitched. Were they so stupid that they abandoned the belief in Jesus which brought them the Spirit, to achieve their life-targets by law-keeping, or performance?
Were God's gifts of His spirit, and His miracles all for nothing?

They should take Abraham as a test case, and see how his faith in God has made everyone who lives by faith children of Abraham, put right with God, and put in the way of blessing.

Law-keeping is not a faith-based method of becoming right with God. In fact, our sinful failures to keep God's law have brought us under a curse, for which Jesus has become a curse for us, to redeem us to God. In this non-Jewish, non-law-based way, Gentiles enter into God's promise of the Spirit.

The way of faith and promise is confirmed by how wills and / or covenants operate. They normally involve two parties, and both parties have to keep up the conditions. God's promise was based on Himself, as one party, and on Christ, as one party, so in His grace God's promise came to Abraham. The law served the useful purpose of defining sin and declaring all men sinners, until Jesus came to deliver ad give life. The Law was like a prison officer, with a custodial role until we were justified. Now our keynote as Christians is a sense of belonging – to God, to Christ, to each other, and to God's salvation-history. This breaks down a lot of man-made barriers.

CHAPTER 7.

BEWITCHED, BOTHERED AND BEWILDERED
Galatians chapter 3 verses 1-9.

In the opening two chapters Paul has been defending his position **personally** as an apostle, and his message of how people can get right with God through faith in Christ alone. He has closed off the possibilities of any additions or alterations to this Gospel by false teachers, and has shown that his message has been confirmed by the Jerusalem church leaders in the test case of Titus, an uncircumcised Greek. Paul rounded off chapter two by showing that righteousness is matching the character of God, and how God can produce a 'not guilty' verdict on us because the Lord Jesus has died in our place for our sins, and there is a kind of righteousness transfer possible for us. Then he showed that the Christian life involves not only in a change of identity and a change of personality, but a change of dependency in our lives.

Chapters 1 and 2 defended Paul's authority **personally.** The false teachers had not only made Paul a target for their scurrilous remarks and critical comments, but they had blown the Galatian believers off course, so in chapters 3 and 4 Paul moves on to explain his Gospel **doctrinally** in a series of arguments. The first two of them are found in chapter 3 verses 1-10, the argument from the Galatians' experience, and the argument from Abraham's experience. Verse 1 reveals the **truth of the Gospel as Visible,** and verses 2-10 reveals the **truth of the Gospel as Viable,** in three different ways: Personally (verses 2-5), Historically (verses 6-7) , and Prophetically(verses 8-10). Let's listen to this section of the letter in the Message version: 'You crazy Galatians! Did somebody put a hex on you? Have you taken leave of your senses? Something crazy has happened, for it's obvious that you no longer have the crucified Jesus in clear focus in your lives. His sacrifice on the Cross was certainly set before you clearly enough.

Let me put this question to you. How did your new life begin? Was it by working your heads off to please God? Or was it by responding to God's Message to you? Are you going to continue this craziness? For only crazy people would think they could complete by heir own efforts what was begun by God. If you weren't smart enough or strong enough to begin it, how could you suppose you could perfect it? Did you go through this painful learning process for nothing? It is not yet a total loss, but it certainly will be if you keep this up!

Answer this question: Does the God who lavishly provides you with his own presence, His Holy Spirit, working things in your lives you could never do for yourselves, does He do these things because of your strenuous moral striving OR because you trust Him to do them in you? Don't these things happen among you just as they happened with Abraham? He believed God, and that act of belief turned into a life that was right with God.

Is it not obvious to you that persons who put their trust in Christ (not persons who put their trust in the law!) are, like Abraham, children of faith? It was all laid out beforehand in Scripture that God would set things right with non-Jews by faith. Scripture anticipated this in the promise to Abraham : 'all nations will be blessed in you.' So those who live by faith are blessed along with Abraham, who lived by faith – this is no new doctrine! And that means that anyone who tries to live by his own effort, independent of God, is doomed to failure. Scripture backs this up: 'Utterly cursed is every person who fails to carry out every detail written in the Book of the law.'

We are looking at Galatians chapter 3 verses 1-10, in which the apostle Paul moves from a largely **personal** defence of his gospel and his role as an apostle, to a mainly **doctrinal** defence. In the opening verses, he not only doubts the spirituality of the Galatians, he also doubts their sanity! The various translations call them 'crazy', 'senseless', 'idiotic', 'foolish', 'stupid'. A cultured Englishman would say they were 'out of their tiny minds'.

The TV interviewer of the former members of the Branch Davidian cult in Waco Texas was very direct in his questioning. David Koresh and his followers had destroyed themselves in a fire. 'Why did you ever listen to such a crazy man? How could you believe such nonsense?'

Paul is no less direct in questioning the Galatian Christians here. Perhaps Professor Lorimer's New Testament in Scots is best 'My puir glaikit Galatians'. Paul asks them in 'The Message' 'who has put a hex on you?', and the New Living Translation asks 'what magician has put an evil spell on you?'. The New International Version asks 'who has bewitched you', and Professor Barclay translates 'who has put the evil eye on you'. I think we catch the drift. Is their irrational behaviour the result of witchcraft? We know that belief in the evil eye goes back to at least ancient Egypt, and at the latest 3000BC. Such belief became widespread and persistent.   Parents used to protect their children from lingering looks from adults, and in the Middle Ages in Britain such unwarranted staring could pinpoint a person as a witch or a person involved in the black arts. Some trace the use of eye-shadow and lipstick as means of protection from incursions of evil into the eyes and mouth respectively. Greek letter-writers expressed fear of spells cast by the evil eye, and often included sentences like 'above all I pray that you may be in good health unharmed by the evil eye,' etc.

Jean-Jacques Rousseau heralded his account of the French Revolution with the sentence: 'Man is born free, but is everywhere in chains'. Paul was worried that he could hear the clank of the chains in the lives of the Galatian Christians, who looked as if they were about to lose their new-found freedom in Christ because of a bewitching spell which was leading them into their old bondage and trouble.

If their trouble came through the eye, and through some individually mesmeric preacher (the 'who' in the question is singular in the Greek text and may hint at some strong-minded leader among the false teachers), Paul reminds them first of all that their initial reception of the Gospel was also **VISUAL.** William Barclay translates the text 'before whose very eyes Jesus Christ was placarded upon His Cross'.

We have quoted before the Arab saying that 'he is the best teacher who can turn the ear into an eye.' Walter Hansen writes: 'Paul's preaching was like an artist painting a picture with words, or putting up a public poster for all to see.' The usage of this word 'placarded' means both ideas, painter and bill-poster, are permissible for us to understand the meaning. Paul's preaching was so graphic and visual, it had a lasting and powerful effect on the hearers.

One of my friends became a Christian through listening to the teaching of Dr Martyn Lloyd-Jones in his Friday evening Bible Class in Westminster Chapel, London. As he presented Romans 3 verse 25 'God presented him (that is, Jesus) as a sacrifice of atonement through faith in His blood', my pal Bob said he could 'see it written in the ceiling'!

On the written side of the meaning, in the ancient world, before the advent of newspapers, the town centre was the place to post public notices. The Greek word 'prographein' used here was used of a father notifying the public that he would no longer be responsible for his son's debts. In contrast with the hidden rituals of the Old Testament Holy of Holies in the Tent-shrine and the Temple, Jesus was crucified publicly outside the city wall of Jerusalem. In the days of the French Revolution, a group of ladies called 'les tricoteuses' ('the knitters') used to bring their knitting and gather round the guillotine to witness the slaughter. It was the same in the time of our Lord. There were always spectators at a crucifixion. The Bible says: 'and sitting down they watched Jesus there.' It was so public. Paul says, in effect, to the Galatians 'My preaching made the crucifixion of the Lord Jesus so central and public, so **VISIBLE.** How can you forget it so quickly, and go after the false teachers?'

May I ask you as a reader whether you have ever had a vision or a conception of the Crucifixion of Jesus like the Galatians had when they stepped into the freedom and light of Christ's gospel ? When I was a boy in primary school, I had never been to church, but I used to wonder at the words of W.W. How's children's hymn we sang in school assembly at Easter:

'I sometimes think about the Cross, and shut my eyes, and try to see
The cruel nails, and crown of thorns, and Jesus crucified for me.

But even could I see Him die, I could but see a little part
Of that great love which, like a fire,

Is always burning in His heart.'

Although Jesus was the greatest Teacher of all time, it is not the Sermon on the Mount which saves us, it is the Cross on the hill. The symbol of Christianity is a Cross, not a chalkboard. We've said before that the Gospels are the most lop-sided biographies ever written. 37% of Mark's Gospel (253 verses out of 677) deal with the last week in our Lord's life. This tells us that the Cross is central in the Good News of Jesus. The only safe place for us to be in the matter of our salvation is kneeling at that cross in repentance and faith, totally dependent on God's free and sovereign grace in Christ. If that is the case, to return to Paul's argument here in Galatians 3 verse 2 'I would like to learn just one thing from you: Did you receive the Spirit by observing the law, or by believing what you heard.'

Their experience of the Gospel was **Viable** personally only by knowing God's divine power surging through them as they were born again by the Spirit of God as a result of their response of faith. If that were the case, he argues in verses 3 and 4, why are you now depending on human effort to complete the job? Are you looking to the Sorcerer or the Saviour? In verse 4 he invites them to review the agonising process of giving up their superstitious ways to follow Jesus. I guess that there are similar superstitious practices to those which held the Galatians in their iron grip, right here in Britain today, and in Scotland which has known so much of God's blessing in the past. In every town and city there are psychic fairs where you can a have your fortune told and buy stones or crystals to rub. There is a proliferating market on the web for all kinds of superstitious good luck devices. Every souvenir shop is selling images of various gods of different religions.. When I responded to a request to conduct a funeral (in Scotland), the first thing I saw when I went into their main living room was a six-foot wooden statue of a Red Indian (or native American if you wish). The walls were festooned with incantations and prayers and the family were deeply into North American shamanism – in Inverness!

Paul says to the Galatians – and to us 'do you think you will come to know God by the indwelling Spirit of God making Jesus an increasing reality to you, or by all this superstitious mumbo-jumbo'. The particular obsession imparted through the false teachers was a slavish loyalty to performance which followed Jewish ceremony, and law-keeping. It was as big a shock to me as the Galatians' behaviour was to Paul, that people in Britain would give credibility to some of this stuff, and prefer to use the lovely Name of Jesus as a swear word. The Galatians had not only witnessed the Lord Jesus Christ placarded before them in the Apostolic preaching of the Cross, but they had seen the viability of their faith in Him as they witnessed confirmatory signs and wonders among them. God had been undeniably at work among them. Chapter 3 verse 5 asks 'Does God give you His Spirit and work miracles among you because you observe the law, or because you believe what you heard? To sum up, Paul asks them and us, 'What's wrong with your eyes?' in verse 1, and in verses 2-5 'What's wrong with your experience?'

Their vision had gone wonky, so Paul reminds them in verse 4 of the view of their receiving the Spirit, in verse 5 of God bestowing the Spirit, and verses 6-9 of Scripture confirming the Spirit. Their faith was not only personally but historically viable.

I suppose there are church-goers today who think that their performance will stockpile merit for them with God. Like the Galatians, they think that anything other than a penitent heart and a trusting soul will win God's favour. Martin Luther said that the establishing of the Law is the abolishing of the Gospel. If performance rather than faith is the ground of their acceptance with God, they might as well have their name on a sausage roll as a church roll! Paul is trying manfully to re-establish the bridgehead God had made into the hearts of the Galatian believers. He takes on the false teachers on their own ground by introducing the test case of Abraham (he does the same in his Letter to the Romans, chapter 4.) Abraham was regarded by these Judaisers as the Father of the Faithful and the fountainhead of their faith. In verses 6 and 7, Paul invites them to consider Abraham, and he takes up the Old Testament text to demonstrate that their faith in Christ is **historically** as well as **personally** viable. 'Abraham believed God, and it was credited to him as righteousness.' Elsewhere Paul argues that Abraham's exercise of faith was prior to the rite of circumcision he followed, and the giving of the Law through Moses. He also argues in Galatians (chapter 3 verse 29) that those who believe are following Abraham, for whom faith was a priority and a prerequisite, which in the days of the patriarch Abraham was 'credited to him as righteousness'. In other words, Paul is saying that faith is number one in God's ledger of acceptance, and this is what the Galatians exercised when they trusted Christ, so why do they need anything else? They, like Abraham, are children of God, through faith.

Walter Hansen discusses the whole issue of Christian identity arising out of this passage. He tells how Christians in Singapore are painfully aware of negative references to 'Christian/Western' values'. When Chinese people in Singapore become Christians (as they are in large numbers there), must they abandon their Chinese identity and adopt Western values, lifestyle and identity.

Brother Walter Hansen compares this crisis to that faced by the Galatians: 'they were adrift in no man's land between the pagan temples and the Jewish synagogues. They belonged to neither. They had abandoned the gods and religious practices of the temples. But they did not attend the Jewish synagogues nor were they welcome there, even though they read the Jewish scriptures and believed in a Jewish messiah. As new Christians without a clear sense of identity they were easily persuaded that if they acquired a Jewish identity they would belong to the people of God...'

Paul in this passage defines their identity. He compares them to Abraham, verse 6, then he identifies them as children of Abraham on the basis of a common family characteristic, verse 7. He confirms that identification by quoting Old Testament Scripture verse 8, and on that basis he includes them in the family blessing. Our own sense of identity can be clarified and strengthened as we trace the steps in this identification process.

We are nearing the end of this section of Galatians chapter 3 in which we have been looking at the amazed apostle Paul, shaken to the core by the Galatians' defection to the false teachers. They are behaving, as Professor Lorimer says, in a glaikit way as if some odd spell had been put on them. Paul demonstrated in this chapter that their faith in Christ had been both visible, and viable in three ways- personally, historically in the test case of Abraham, and thirdly, **prophetically.**

If the Christian Gospel is no flash-in-the-pan faith, then you would expect a certain integrity and consistency in the unfolding drama of redemption, so Paul is able to quote from God's prophecy to a man who lived about 1800 years before Christ that in him all the families of the earth would be blessed, or bless themselves, however you take the translation.

If God is known as the Alpha and the Omega, the first and final letters of the Greek alphabet, then it stands to reason He knows the whole story of the unfolding of world and personal history from beginning to end. This is the God whom we are called to trust. The death of His Son was no tragic accident. Jesus was not the victim of circumstances, nor was his trial a mere blip on the screen of Roman justice. His death was the climax of human history, and when Jesus cried out 'it is finished' on the Cross, he meant it. We like the Galatians can stake our decision-making, our career and marriage/family choices and our whole future on it.. We can be sure by faith in Christ alone we are part of God's family and part of His salvation history! What a message! Believe it! Grasp it! Hold on to it! Roll it under your tongue like a sweetie every day you live!

QUESTIONS FOR DISCUSSION
CHAPTER 3 v 1-9

1. Can Christians be 'bewitched'? How should we relate to the occult?

2. Does 'clear portrayal' provide a definition of good preaching? What are the elements of good preaching?

3. Is 'the age of miracles' past in the Christian church? (2 v 5). Discuss.

4. What links do we have to the Old Testament in general, and to Abraham in particular?

CHAPTER 8.

SALVATION, LAW, AND PROMISE.
GALATIANS CHAPTER 3 verses 10-24.

In this chapter we are looking at the title 'Salvation, Law and Promise', and we'll see again the liberating power of Christ's Good News, in Galatians chapter 3 verses 10-15. Here it is in Peterson's translation The Message': "Anyone who tries to live by his own effort, independent of God, is doomed to failure. Scripture backs this up: 'Utterly cursed is every person who fails to carry out every detail written in the book of the law.' The obvious impossibility of carrying out such a moral programme should make it plain that no one can sustain a relationship with God that way. The person who lives in right relationship with God does it by embracing what God arranges for him. Doing things for God is the opposite of entering into what God does for you. Habakkuk had it right: 'the person who believes God is set right by God - and that's the real life.' Rule-keeping does not naturally evolve into living by faith, but: only perpetuates itself into more and more rule-keeping, a fact observed in Scripture: 'the one who does these things (rule-keeping) continues to live by them.' Christ redeemed us from that self-defeating, cursed life by absorbing it completely into Himself. Do you remember the Scripture that says: 'Cursed is everyone that hangs on a tree?' That is what happened when Jesus was nailed to the Cross. He became a curse, and at the same time dissolved the curse. And now because of that the air is cleared and we can see that Abraham's blessing is present and available for non-Jews too. We are ALL able to receive God's life, His Spirit, in and with us by believing -just the way Abraham received it.'

In the course of his letter to the Galatian Christians, Paul had raised a number of important issues. For example, how did he become an apostle? Where did he get his authority? Did his Gospel pass the test of soundness and orthodoxy? Was simply trusting Jesus enough to put people right with God? How did his Gospel stand up to a test case: like Titus, an uncircumcised

Greek? Did Paul get his teaching approach by 'going to school' on the Jerusalem apostles? Or was he operating, like a loose cannon, independently of Peter and James, for example? How did holding his belief system affect his relationship with his fellow-Christians? He had also attempted to answer these issues. He was commissioned directly by the Risen Lord Jesus, and so ranked with the other apostles who were eye-witnesses. He had spent time alone with God to rethink everything he had been taught and had learned as a Jewish religious expert. His Gospel was rooted and grounded in the sovereign and free grace of God, free from the taint of human achievement or performance. Everyone, Jew and Gentile, were accepted on the same basis without in any way kow-towing to Jewish ritual, ceremony food laws or calendar. He had established strong fellowship links with the Jerusalem church leaders, and there had been a clear agreement that Paul's first priority was to preach the Good News to Gentiles, with their blessing and prayer support. It is actually good for us as twenty-first century people, to go over these fundamental points in relation to the church today, and see that the basics are still valid.

Paul is bringing his doctrine of salvation by grace under the searchlight, to see what comes out of the shadows. In these verses, he shows that salvation comes by the blessing of faith rather than the curse of the law, (verses 10-12), that salvation comes through Christ rather than law, that is Christ's Person rather than my performance (verses 13-14), that salvation comes by Promise rather than law (verses 15-18) and through the deliverance of faith rather than the misery of imprisonment (verses 19-25). In this section Paul swings round from the argument based on experience - theirs and Abraham's - to the argument based on Scripture. They had seen personally and historically and prophetically that God was committed to blessing them, and Abraham and the Gentiles, through faith. Faith connected Abraham to Gentiles in Paul's day, just as it connects him to us nowadays. He now takes on the Judaising false teachers using their own style and approach, using Old Testament proof-texts to back up his argument. In verse 10 he shows them that their coat is hanging on a shaky peg if they are hoping to please God by keeping His law. God's standard is 100% or else! They must not be like a tight-rope walker across Niagara Falls , expecting a second chance if they fall! If they or we connect ourselves to performance, even one failure brings us into the curse of the law rather than the blessing of Abraham. In verse 11, Paul shows that salvation must come on a different basis than perfect performance from imperfect people. The Habakkuk way was living by faith daily, that is, steadfastly. The law-keeping was based on actions, and as Paul shows in verse 11, the promise of life in Leviticus was useless, because the people concerned were unable to perform perfectly. Therefore Jesus Christ becomes our only hope. He has lived a perfect life, and he has taken on the curse of the law by becoming a curse for us. See verse 13: 'Christ redeemed us from the curse of the law by becoming a curse for us, by dying on a tree'. This action was a combination of the substitutionary and the penal. Jesus died in my place and took on the penalty of my sin.

The word 'redeemed' is used in verse 13 and verse 14. In Paul's time, slavery was a vital and permanent feature of life in the Roman Empire. Somewhere between a quarter and a third of the population were slaves. The imagery here is that of a slave being bought at the slave-market and set free. It has come into focus in our society just now (2007) because of the two hundredth anniversary of the Act of Parliament which freed British slaves in the West Indies. The emancipation of slaves came through the constant campaigning of William Wilberforce, a converted card-sharp and a gambler, MP for Hull, who called himself a 'moderate Calvinist'. The 14000 British slaves were given Ivory Coast to resettle, with its capital Freetown. My own early connections with redemption are related to the pawn-shop. In my youth in Possilpark, Glasgow, there were a few pawnshops around - Quigley and McManus in Possilpark, and there was one of the Garscube Road with a sign 'Are you like the baker, needing dough? We lend money, don't you know?' As a family, we were needing dough fairly regularly, especially on Thursdays, and I was sent with a brown paper parcel to the pawnshop. My father's going-to-football suit was the only item in the house which could be used. I would go into the cubicle with the squeaky door and hand over his suit in exchange for a pawn ticket. Then on Friday when my mother got paid, I was sent with the pawn ticket to redeem my father's suit. In Gospel terms I learned later that Jesus had paid the price by dying on the Cross to redeem me from the slavery of sin and Satan. Therefore I shared the sense of being 'born free' which the Galatian Christians had, and which is the birthright of every Christian. Christ has redeemed us, from law as a way of salvation, which had actually brought us under the curse which failure brings (verse 13), and for blessing (verse 14), so that we can share in the blessing Abraham knew (verse 14).

In the ensuing section, Paul moves swiftly and skilfully to promise rather than law as the basis of our salvation (verses 15-18).

The law of God was terribly important to the Jews and to the false teachers who seemed to follow Paul around, snapping like mongrels at his heels...The special part of God's revelation they were interested in was the Torah (which means 'direction' rather than 'instruction'), sometimes called the Pentateuch, the first five books of the Old Testament part of the Christian Bible (Genesis to Deuteronomy). The Jews sometimes called it 'the five-fifths of the Law'. They knew the core of that Law, which they believed was handed down by the angels, was the 10 Commandments. They had embellished and added to the 10 Commandments another 603 commandments to be kept. There were three different kinds of Old Testament Law - the civil law relating to occupation of Israel, the ceremonial law which was the rule of sacrifice enshrined in the Book of Leviticus, and the moral law, epitomised in the 10 commandments. For many modern Christians, the only valid and binding part now is the moral law, since the civil law related to the settlement in Canaan, and the ceremonial law or the law of sacrifices, has been superseded because of Christ's death.

In this section, Paul shows the importance of God's promise, and how promise supersedes law in His purposes. The word 'promise' occurs frequently in these verses. The section has caused a lot of problems, but well do our best to simplify the meaning. Some Bible teachers think their task is to bamboozle and lose their students, in order to blind them with their erudition! Other teachers like to codify, simplify and organise the truths they are teaching. I would rather be the second kind of teacher, and pray to this end! In verses 15-18 Paul uses a few curious arguments. In verse 15 he is probably writing about a will, rather than a covenant. In our legal system, people can change their will, altering their wishes and promises by adding codicils, or making a new one. In Greek law, a will once written could not be revoked or altered. If a man's will cannot be altered, how much more is God's will unchangeable. In verse 16 he hangs his argument on a singular 'offspring' rather than a plural 'offsprings', which illustrates incidentally how seriously New Testament writers took the Old Testament text, and how Paul was able to relate it to Christ as representative man here. The promise related initially to the Promised Land of Canaan, but it was ultimately wider than that. In verse 18 he underlines the kindness of God in that the law, given 430 years after the promise, did not and could not wipe out the promise, but was like the promise given to Abraham, a gift of God's grace. The figure of 430 years given here is a rough number based on Exodus 12 verse 40. In verse 19, Paul pre-empts an objector by answering the questions 'Why do we need the law?', and 'Are you not short-circuiting Moses and the Law here, Paul?' Paul believes in the validity of law, just as he would argue for the validity of a mirror to show us that our face is dirty, and requiring the remedial action of soap and water. So we need Exodus (the mirror) AND Leviticus (the soap and water.)

The writer Paul is defending his thumping endorsement of God's Promise over God's law, and is trying to show that he believes God's law is a good thing, even if law-keeping performance is not a valid path to salvation. For each one of us, it is good to emphasise that we can no more please God by being good and doing good than we can lift ourselves up by pulling at our own shoe laces. The force of gravity is like the force of sin in our lives, pulling us down, and the only way to God is by grace through faith. The old acrostic for faith was 'forsaking all I trust Him'. Bishop Stephen Neill points out that 'the promise came to Abraham first-hand and the law comes to the people third-hand God-the angels- Moses the Mediator- the people.' God's law was a means of grace to show us the need for cleansing until the Mediator came (see verse 19-20) . He argues in verse 20 that mediation requires two parties. The law is only valid if both parties are in agreement. If God is sole partner then the promise stands clean, absolute and unconditional. And His grace persists at all times.

What therefore is Paul's evaluation of law? Is it against the promises of God? He says it is useful to put down a marker on transgressions. In Romans 7 he shows that it may have the side-effect of stirring up sin, like a sweeping brush, which has a cleansing function, but may stir up dirt in a room. In verses 24 and 25 he uses two images of the law that are very helpful. The first one is the imagery of the prison guard, and the second is that of the escort, or custodian. Before the sunshine of the life of faith broke into us, we were like prisoners locked in a prison cell, and the law was our custodian. The older translation of 'schoolmaster' was misleading, for the emphasis here seems to be discipline rather than education, even if every good schoolmaster has discipline as part of the package for the student. The law was like a restraining guardian, keeping us under control until we experienced gospel freedom. In the Roman Empire, sometimes trusted slaves were put in charge of children's welfare, and acted as escorts to and from school as part of their duties. Educated slaves (sometimes captured Greeks for example) were given custodial responsibilities as far as supervising homework, or even helping with tutorial work. In verse 25, Paul says the glad reality of the indwelling Christ through the Holy Spirit, means that we no longer need the services of our 'law-custodian.' Maturity at last! In his Hymn to Love in 1 Corinthians 13, Paul uses the imagery of the schoolroom. When I was a child' he says I talked like child, I thought like a child, I reasoned like a child. When I became a man, I put away childish things.' All good schools prepare us for real living, but one day the unreality of the classroom is over, we pack away our schoolbooks in our desks, and go out to face the world and real life.

What can we learn from this passage? Paul's timeline from Abraham through Moses to Jesus reminds us of God's careful planning of history. It also teaches us that the Old Testament has a lot to teach us. This theme will be taken up again in the next section, and in chapter 4. Far too many Christians ignore the Old Testament, which Martin Luther called 'the crib in which the Christ-child is laid.' They are New Testament Christians rather than Bible Christians. They are like people breathing with only one lung, or rowers in a boat with only one oar. They fail to see the big picture, which used to be enshrined in a children's song: 'He's a mighty big God, isn't He?' It is so easy to miss the big picture in our understanding of God and His grace. Listen to John Stott: 'Here the apostle Paul, with a breadth of vision which leaves us far behind, brings together Abraham, Moses and Jesus Christ. In eight short verses he spans about 2000 years. He surveys practically the whole Old Testament landscape. He presents it like a mountain range whose highest peaks are Abraham and Moses and whose Everest is Jesus Christ. He shows how God's promise to Abraham was confirmed by Moses and fulfilled in Christ.'

The second comment is that we need to stop fiddling with the Bible, and abandon the Jack Horner method of interpreting it. A lot of preachers and so-called or self-styled experts just 'put in a thumb and pull out a plum and say what a good boy am I.' We need more than just a few lectures at a Bible College or a few expensive courses master-minded by some cliche-laden Christian who is 'into prophecy' or 'into counselling'. We need to spend lots of time on our knees with our Bibles open before God. Today there as excellent helps for those who want to understand and explain the whole sweep of Biblical revelation. The need of the hour in the churches is not better techniques but holier Christians who live each day in closer touch with God through prayer and Bible study.

The third comment is that the best thing for us is that we need to tremble before God's law before we experience the glorious exhilaration of His Gospel. The Puritans said that we needed the needle of the law before the scarlet thread of the Gospel. As Paul says in this section, the law of God has an important role in our lives. Remember what Jesus said 'he who is forgiven much, loves much.' If we have an acute awareness of the hopelessness of our awful state before God before we are converted, then we'll love Jesus all the more and want to give ourselves to Him in a spirit of constant gratitude every day of our lives. As you are reading this chapter today, do you realise that the Bible teaches that there is a heaven to gain and a hell to shun? Did you know that most of the teaching on hell in the New Testament comes from the lips of the Lord Jesus Christ. Did you know that if you do not have saving faith in Jesus the Son of God, you are condemned already? Did you know that one day every knee shall bow to Christ an every tongue confess that He is Lord, willingly or unwillingly? And do you know that God made you for Himself, and that you will never know true happiness until that God-shaped blank in your life is filled with the Lord Jesus and His Holy Spirit? Would you believe me if I told you that there is unspeakable joy in believing and following Christ, and pleasures at His right hand for evermore? Life without Him is mere existence. Reality comes, like the schoolboy picture in 1 Corinthians 13, when we step out and leap into the loving arms of a Saviour who shed His blood and gave His life for you and me.

The fourth observation is that comparing the law of God with the Gospel of God is like comparing electric light with the brightness of sunlight. Law heightens our sense of sin, but it has severe limitations. William Barclay suggests that we cannot be condemned for doing a wrong thing if we did not know that it was a wrong thing. Therefore part of the function of the law is to define sin. But while the law can and does define sin, it can do nothing at all to cure sin. He says: There is at one and the same time the strength and weakness of the law. The strength of the law is that it defines sin; its weakness is that it can do nothing to cure sin. It is like a doctor who is an expert in diagnosis, but who is helpless to clear up the trouble he has diagnosed. The Old Testament measures set out in the sacrificial system were interim until Jesus came to put away sin by the sacrifice of Himself. Physically, there was darkness around His Cross for three hours. Spiritually, the Gospel sun shines in all its splendour from his Cross. Paul personalises it in his Corinthian letter. The same God, who commanded the light to shine out of darkness, has shone in our hearts to give the knowledge of the glory of God in the face of Jesus Christ. A child told her daddy as he carried her up into the bedroom: 'switch off the darkness, daddy!' God has done that for us through Christ. Paul says elsewhere 'God was in Christ, reconciling the world to himself.'

Fifthly, (I find that difficult to say!), Paul's Gospel has an effect on sociology as well as theology. The time-line Abraham-Moses-Jesus illustrates the inclusiveness of Christianity which stood in contrast to the exclusivism of Judaism in the time of the New Testament. Conversion to Judaism automatically implied nationalising as well. In Galatians, Paul is urging a de-nationalising of the people of God. Paul was wanting Jews who became Christian believers to relinquish their commitment to the law which defined who they were. Today the Christian faith is for everyone, and the Gospel can reach people without distinction. Christian churches should not and cannot construct barriers to full fellowship and service for 'some kinds' of people. That is why there is a religious revival among gypsies in Eastern Europe and a welcoming attitude from Christians towards asylum seekers in Britain.

Finally (recognising the difficulties of preachers saying or writing the word 'finally'!), the word translated 'inheritance' in chapter 3 verse 18 will reappear in a different guise in chapter 4 verse 1, where Paul argues from the basis that a Christian is an 'heir' of salvation. Alan Cole, a good Australian brother, says: 'In Scripture, the inheritance is inseparable from the gift of the Spirit, the 'pledge' or 'engagement ring' guaranteeing our inheritance in Ephesians chapter 1 verse 4....it is hard to avoid the conclusion that Paul is also thinking, in a specifically New Testament sense, of the gift of the Spirit in Galatians 3 verse 14.....for the believer, 'grace' is Christ.'
The Gospel promises us a great inheritance, and we can start living on its benefits here and now as well as then and there. What a blessing!

In the next chapter we hope to be looking at Galatians 3 verses 26-28 under the theme of 'Alienation and Belonging'.

QUESTIONS FOR DISCUSSION.

3 v 10-24.

1. How does the law of God catch us out?

2. How can Jesus offer us freedom and blessing instead of the curse of the law ?

3. Discuss the link Paul makes between the covenant with Abraham, and the Lord Jesus?

4. What use is the law of God to us?   Discuss.

5. What TWO images does Paul use in verses 23 and verse 24 to describe the function of law?

CHAPTER 9.

ALIENATION AND BELONGING
Galatians Chapter 3 verses 25-29.

In this chapter, we move on to the end of Galatians chapter 3, under the title 'Alienation and Belonging', verses 26-29. Here they are in the New International Version: 'You are all sons of God through faith in Christ Jesus. For all of you who were baptized into Christ have clothed yourselves with Christ. There is neither Jew nor Greek, slave or free, male nor female, for you are all one in Christ Jesus. If you belong to Christ, then you are Abraham's seed, and heirs according to the promise.'

We live in a world characterised by alienation and isolation. Let me give a few illustrations. Jean Forbes lived in an apartment block in America. Some bad characters came to her door, robbed her, stabbed her, and she cried for help but bled to death at her doorstep. Police enquiries revealed that a total of 46 people had heard her cries, but no-one helped. They didn't want to be involved, for different reasons. One of the reasons people are not happy with supermarkets is the feeling of alienation they foster. Have you ever tried to have a conversation with someone at a check-out? You'll probably manage 30 seconds if you're lucky! Have you ever travelled on the London Underground, squashed against someone you've never met in your life before, among thousands who are able to travel without ever looking anyone directly in the eye. Gordon Jackson, the Scottish actor who starred in 'Upstairs, Downstairs' boasted that he had lived in a leafy suburb in London for three years without ever engaging anyone in conversation. Personal stereos and their modern equivalents effectively isolate people from their fellow human beings. A lady I knew attended a church coffee morning for about three months without anyone ever speaking to her. At home, because of the advent of central heating, carpets and other home comforts, some families spent most of their time isolated in their rooms, and rarely sit at the meal table as family.

The newspapers are full of it, and everyone is outraged when some old person is found dead at home after days, or even weeks. How dare they disgrace the district! Jean Toomer, a black intellectual, wrote : 'I saw myself as if on a boat which the nations would allow to put up at no port. I could come in for food and supplies. This done, I'd have to put out to sea again....never having a harbour which I could call my own, never knowing port in which I could come to rest- always at sea...by order of the government of the universe.'

In the cartoon series 'Peanuts', Charlie Brown and his friends were discussing where people feel out of place – libraries, concert halls, football grounds and so on. Someone asks Charlie Brown where he feels out of place, and he replies 'The Universe.'
Against a rising stream of alienation, the Christian Gospel, and the Letter to the Galatians shouts 'This needn't be how you live! You belong! You belong! You belong!'.

The Christian Good News is that we need not and dare not live in miserable isolation. God made us to mingle, and know that we belong.
Paul says in Galatians chapter 3 verse 24: 'You are all sons of God through faith in Christ Jesus', so first of all. :
A. YOU BELONG TO GOD. This relates to the **SONSHIP YOU BEAR.**
The Christian view is that we were made in the image of God, and bear His likeness. We are spiritual beings bearing something of the dignity of His character. Genesis is the book of beginnings, and sets out foundational principles which are perpetually valid. Genesis chapter 2 verse 7 says: 'the Lord God made man from the dust of the ground and breathed into his nostrils the breath of life, and the man became a living being.' This special endowment of the breath of God sets humankind apart from the animal creation. Humanity has come from the hand of a good God. Therefore God is our Father in the general sense that as our Creator the breath we now draw is a moment-by-moment renewal of the gift of life from Him. One of Augustine's favourite texts was John 15 verse 5 'without me you can do nothing'.
Despite the evolutionists claims, we're not glorified monkeys:

'Said the professor to the protoplasm
'Twixt thee and me there's an awful chasm;
It's hard to see when I look, son,
To think I finished what you begun...'

Augustine distinguished between the natural human faculties given to man by God's endowment, and additional and special gifts of God's grace. Alister McGrath writes concerning Augustine's view: ' God does not leave us as we are naturally, incapacitated through sin and unable to redeem ourselves, but gives us grace in order that we may be healed, forgiven and restored.'
The Bible makes it clear that we can know God as Father in two different ways. We can acknowledge Him generally as Creator, and we can believe in Him as Saviour. This brings us into a special relationship with Him.
In the wonderful panoramic view of Jesus as the Logos of God in John chapter 1, the writer in verses 11 -13 says:
'He came to that which was His own, but His own did not receive Him. Yet to all who received Him, to those who believed in His name, He gave the right to become children of God – children born not of natural descent, nor of human decision or a husband's will, but born of God.'
One of the privileges of this special relationship is that we can look up into God's face and call Him 'Abba', one of the Aramaic fragments retained in the New Testament. It was the term used by small children speaking to their Daddy. It is a word of intimate relationship. The German theologian Joachim Jeremias wrote a lovely little book entitled 'The Central Message of the New Testament', and built a case that this four-letter word, (which you can say without teeth!), is at the heart of the Gospel. This is the sonship which Christians bear –You belong to God, through faith in Christ Jesus. Are you sure you belong to God as Saviour in this special way?

We've looked at the fact that Christians Belong to God – this is the Sonship we Bear. In verse 27 Paul writes: 'for all of you who were baptized into Christ have clothed yourselves with Christ.'
B You Belong to Christ. This relates to **the Clothing you**

Wear.
In this verse, Paul refers to baptism, a vivid image of incorporation whether his readers were thinking of Jewish proselyte baptism or Christian baptism. Early Christian baptism was a dramatised salvation. It is the faith rather than the baptism which unites us with Christ. The whole drama of it indicates the end of one relationship and the beginning of another. It is a picture of the passage from spiritual death to spiritual life. Baptism is the outward and visible sign of an inward and spiritual act which has already taken place. Faith and baptism together signify identification and incorporation into Christ. In the Old Testament book of Judges, chapter 6 verse 34, the Spirit of God 'puts on' Gideon like a garment. In Christian baptism, the candidate used to put on new white robes. Alan Cole writes: 'The use of 'stripping ' and 'putting on' may derive from the undressing before baptism, and the subsequent dressing in clean white clothing. But it is peculiarly appropriate as describing a situation where certain habits and qualities have to be laid aside for ever, and a new set assumed.

The Christian, therefore, belongs to Christ, and has put Him on like a garment. Let's extend the imagery a little. In connection with our everyday clothing there are three questions we normally ask. The first one is 'Can I afford it?' In the case of the spotless robe of Christ's righteousness, the answer is 'definitely not'. We are condemned to keep wearing the filthy grave-clothes of our past sinful life. Believing in Christ and belonging to Christ means that we can discard our grave-clothes and put on something more appropriate to new life. The second question we ask is 'Does it fit me?' Putting on Christ like a garment means that our lives fit into the plan and will and pattern God has for our lives. He knows best the path our lives should take, and we share in the Christian experience of transformation set out in Romans chapter 12 verses 2 and 3 : ' Do not conform any longer to the pattern of this world, but be transformed by the renewing of your mind. Then you will be able to test and approve what God's will is – His good, pleasing and perfect will.' The third question we ask- especially the ladies - is 'Does it suit me?' The answer to that is a thumping, resounding 'Yes!' The gift of God is not only the enveloping presence of His Son, and the protection and counsel of His Spirit, but the gift of eternal life which gives us that Christian sparkle, so that we feel at home in Him. This garment definitely fits, and suits.

In this chapter we're looking in our Galatians study at chapter 3 verses 26-28, and learning that in a world of alienation Christians can have a sense of belonging to God and to Christ.
C. You Belong to Each Other, and this relates to **The Freedom You Share.** Paul writes in chapter 3 verse 28 'There is neither Jew nor Greek, slave nor free, male nor female, for you are all one in Christ Jesus.'

Paul lived in a fragmented and divided world. In this verse, he relates Christian fellowship across all the basic boundary walls people build to keep it that way. These were race, rank and sex. Surprise, surprise! The Bible is as relevant today as it was in Paul's time. Let's look at them in some detail and relate what Paul wrote to his own time. In Christ There is **No Distinction of Race.**
'There is neither Jew nor Greek.' God entrusted His message and blessing to the Jews in order that they would pass on the message and the blessing to the whole world. Unfortunately, the saving remnant became the saved remnant and they failed even although in many ways Jews and Gentiles were equal in their need of God's salvation, equal in their inability to achieve it by their own efforts, and equal in the fact that the offer of the Gospel comes to us all freely in Christ. The Gospel can, and has, in Christ created an international fellowship of believers, embracing every race colour and religion. I remember a Pentecostal pastor from the Bronx, leading a tour group in Israel, laughing heartily when I said you could be white, black, yellow or even polka dot, and still belong to this fellowship. I have had fellowship with Christians in France, Italy, Cyprus, Greece, Israel, Kenya, USA and Brazil, and can never get over the 'tingle' and the reality of knowing that we are all one in Christ Jesus.
This was not the case in the first century. The Jews had a prayer of thanksgiving for daily repetition, thanking God that He had not made them a Gentile, a woman, a slave or a prisoner. The

Jews often produced a compound phrase 'Gentile dog', and believed that the Gentiles were created solely to produce fuel for the fires of hell. The Gentiles hated and distrusted the Jews and virtually forced them to live in ghettoes. In Christ, there was also **No Distinction of Rank.**

'neither... slave nor free.' In Paul's world, and that meant Rome's Empire there were anything between a quarter and a third of the population who were slaves. People were made slaves in various ways – purchase, debt, capture in war, and birth. Slaves had no rights, and were at the absolute disposal of masters who were sometimes fickle and unspeakably cruel. Farmers' inventories of their assets would include dumb tools (livestock) and speaking tools (slaves). At one time the Roman Senate debated whether to issue uniforms to slaves, and decided against it, in case they realised how numerous they were, and rose up in revolt. The New Testament letter Paul wrote to Philemon concerned a runaway slave. There were slaves in membership of the Early Church. Only the Gospel could smash down barriers of rank like that. In Christ, there was also **No Distinction of Sex.**

'neither... male nor female' In the Graeco-Roman world generally, women were definitely reckoned to be inferior. The thanksgiving that a Jew was not born a woman was possibly based on the Genesis narrative, with the conclusion drawn that Eve drew Adam into sin, or it may be a 'sigh of relief' prayer that men escaped the pains of childbirth by not being born female. Josephus reckoned 'the woman, says the law, is in all things inferior to the man.' Women were talked about in rude and demeaning ways. They were not to be taught the law, were to tend their children, could be divorced for paltry reasons, but could not obtain divorce, and were considered inferior witnesses in court. Paul takes a sledgehammer to this as unworthy of the Gospel. Phoebe and Priscilla and the treatment by Jesus of women in the Gospels all indicate the abolition of sexual prejudice. Scot McKnight says: ' For those who are in Christ, antagonisms, criticisms, snide remarks, subtle insinuations, and overt prejudices must end, for in Christ male and female are one.'

The distinctions mentioned above are not obliterated. Paul

does not mean that they do not exist, but they should not matter. We recognise people's colour, social background and sexual difference. They are still there, but they do not any longer create any barriers to fellowship.

Paul's agenda would, as it happens take centuries to implement. Today's world is still a divided world. In Britain the gap between rich and poor is widening by the year. The disgusting treatment of women in the sex industry is nauseating, home and overseas. One of my missionary friends described walking through an open air market in Bangkok, Thailand, and seeing young girls for sale like animals in wicker cages. He told me this happened to raise money to pay their family's gambling debts, or the interest on them. Jesus is our only hope, now as then. Only His Gospel can smash down the barriers.

The section is rounded off by these beautiful words: 'All One in Christ Jesus', the motto of the Keswick Convention.

In this chapter we're unpacking the content of Galatians chapter 3 verses 26-29, and seeing that, in an age of alienation, to trust Christ and be born free in Him, means that we belong to God, we belong to Christ, and we belong to each other.

In verse 29, Paul makes a belonging link-up which spans many centuries:

'If you belong to Christ, then you are Abraham's seed, and heirs according to the promise.'

D. You Belong to History, and this relates **to The People You Are.**

We have said before that Abraham was the fountain-head of the Jewish race, but Paul here, and elsewhere, in Romans chapter 4 for example, links Abraham with the modern Christian. Many of our neighbours feel rejected, under-valued, and surplus to modern-day requirements. They sometimes discuss their pain, and wonder whether there is a way by which they'll get out of the cold cave they are in. They feel like corks bobbing about on the surface of an angry ocean, the victims of fate and the playthings of chance. The Gospel is the only answer which makes sense of life, and puts us in context. Trusting in Christ for salvation puts us in step with Abraham. The Germans have a theological word, 'heilsgeschichte', which means 'salvation

–history.' God is working His purposes out, and the principles of His grace which operated in Abraham's life can operate in ours. By trusting in God in the same way as Abraham did, we find ourselves making a leap in the dark into the arms of Jesus. We also learn that our lives are hidden with Christ in God, and we have a security in Him which transcends all circumstances, even apparently bad circumstances. Further, we see ourselves as part of the ongoing plan of God for our own lives, and for the lives of God's people down the centuries. To a Bible reader, history is His Story. Each one of you reading is valuable to God, and can fit into all this. Who could have imagined that a mill-boy from Blantyre, propping up his book on his machine as he worked (DavidLivingstone), or a mill-girl from Dundee, who claimed she was the pawn-shop's best customer (Mary Slessor), would have a major impact on the history and geography of parts of Africa? Who could have guessed that a gaunt rail-splitter from a log cabin (Abraham Lincoln) would become President of the United States, and free the slaves, or a peanut farmer from Georgia in the USA (Jimmy Carter) would become an international peace-maker? God has a work that only you can do! And when you trust in Christ, you fall into line with Abraham, the Father of the Faithful. His faith was like the faith of any twenty-first century Christian. He believed in a God who could bring life from death, on at least two occasions. When God promised him that his wife Sarah would have a child, he believed God (Genesis 15 verse 6). He and Sarah were well beyond the normal age of having children, but Abraham believed that God could produce new life from the deadness of Sarah's womb. Later in life, when God told him to sacrifice his only son Isaac (read Genesis chapter 22), Abraham believed God could raise him from death. Christians also believe in life from the dead, that the Lord Jesus Christ has risen from the dead and is alive for evermore, and by His Spirit and His preachers, offers us new life through His Good News. Therefore by exercising faith, by trusting and believing in the value of Jesus' death and the power of Jesus' life, we are marching in step with Abraham, like foot-soldiers in a great army of faith! What a prospect! And that is not the end, for we are not yet at the end of God's on-going work. We are journeying to a city with foundations, whose Builder and Maker is God. Paul says in this section 'You are Abraham's seed, and heirs according to the promise.'

In the next chapter, we hope to go into Galatians chapter four and see how slaves become sons, and how God's timetable worked out in the birth of Jesus, God's Son.

QUESTIONS FOR DISCUSSION
3 V 25-28

1. How can the 'children of the devil' (see John 8 v 44) become the sons of God? (verse 25 and John 1 v 12) ?

2. Why is clothing a good image of belonging to Christ ?

3. See 3 verse 28. Paul lived in a divided world – so do we. Define and discuss the divisions in today's society.

4. Should 'male and female...all one in Christ Jesus' affect our attitude to church leadership?

5. See 3 v 29. What are we heirs of ?

OUTLINE OF GALATIANS
CHAPTER FOUR.

A child who is an heir has status, and may have wealth, but he has no executive power until father says so. Similarly, we were servants to worldly rules until God's perfect timing brought His Son, naturally born, legally obligated, so that people under legal obligations can be redeemed and released into full rights as sons. Since we now have the status of sons, God grants the indwelling Spirit, whose presence in our lives echoes the name 'Abba'. Therefore we are not slaves but sons, and also heirs.

In your past life, you were in bondage to low-class leadership, but now that you are within the framework of God's knowledge, how can you revert to primitive, enslaving principles. Your calendar-watching tactics make it seem as if I (Paul) have wasted time and effort on you!

Paul recalled his identification with them as an unwell preacher, and their sensitive, loving welcome extended to him. They would have torn out their own eyes to help him. How can telling them the truth have spoiled the relationship?

The false teachers are interested in winning keen camp-followers. Zeal must have a good purpose , and persist even in their leader's absence. He is pained and puzzled, and would love to be with them.

Paul uses an illustration from Abraham's life, and his two sons, one born to a slave woman and one to a free woman. The slave woman's boy was born in the natural way, but the free woman's son was a child who came through God's promise. Paul links up Hagar and the Mount Sinai covenant, bearing children who are slaves. He links up the Heavenly Jerusalem as their free mother, and Isaac with them as children of promise and freedom. The tension between the two sons is resolved by excluding the slave woman and her son.

CHAPTER 10.

FROM SLAVES TO SONS
Galatians Chapter 4 verses 1-11

Paul has defended his status as an apostle, and the content of his Gospel as totally sufficient, solidly based on God's free grace, not requiring any embellishment or addition, with faith in Christ as its sole criterion. He had spent quality time with God in Arabia, filtering his Pharasaic learning through God's filter, and reshaping his theology in that massive brain of his. He had confirmed his message and his mandate to take the Gospel to the Gentiles, with the Jerusalem apostles, and had demonstrated that in a world of alienation it is possible and viable to have a deep sense of belonging as a Christian. Towards the end of chapter three, he had shown that Christians belong to God, belong to Christ, belong to each other, and belong to God's salvation history, walking in step with Abraham, who was also a man of faith, believing, as modern Christians do, in a God who brings life from the dead. Just as God could bring the life of a child of promise, Isaac, from the practically dead womb of Abraham's wife Sarah, so God had raised the Lord Jesus Christ from the dead. Therefore, Christianity is not an antiquarian society, but a living organism. The members of Christian churches do not meet to venerate a dead hero, but to worship the risen Son of God, the Lord Jesus Christ. In his letter to the emperor Trajan around AD 112 (yes, as long ago as that!), Pliny the Governor of the Roman province of Bithynia was describing the behaviour of Christians there. He wrote : 'the sum of their guilt or error had amounted only to this, that on an appointed day, they had been accustomed to meet before daybreak, and to sing hymns to Christ as to a god....' Modern Christians to the same, except they are not as early risers as the good Christians of Bithynia !

Like them, modern Christians are grateful to be reckoned as the sons and heirs of God. The joy of their freedom leads them into praise, especially when they think of their former bondage. They were like people released from prison. In the opening verses of chapter four, Paul tells how they have been set free from the custody of a tutor to be transformed from minors to sons and heirs. Let's hear it in the Message translation:

'Let me show you the implications of this. As long as the heir is a minor, he has no advantage over the slave. Though legally he owns the entire inheritance, he is subject to tutors and administrators until whatever date the father has set for his emancipation. That is the way it is with us: when we were minors, we were just like slaves, ordered around by simple instructions (the tutors and administrators of this world) with no say in the conduct of our own lives. But when the time arrived that was set by God the Father, God sent His Son, born among us of a woman, born under the conditions of the law, so that He might redeem us who have been kidnapped by the law. Thus we have been set free to experience our rightful inheritance....'

Paul has been arguing that the Christians have been born free because they have been delivered from the restrictions of being treated like immature minors, and the reason for that is the birth and the work of redemption accomplished by God's perfect Redeemer. The first feature of this was God's Timing, so that everything was in place for the coming of Christ. The 'time' here was 'chronos' time, or clock time. We would expect the Greek word 'kairos' time to be used, because that means 'opportune' or 'seasonable' time. However, Paul strengthens up the meaning of chronos time here by using the loaded word 'pleroma' which means 'fullness.' The reason may be that some false teachers used the word fullness to indicate the total sum of intermediate stages in the ladder which will get us to God. Paul uses it here to indicate the consummation of God's timing in sending Jesus ! – a good use! Why should the devil have all the good emanations! In Colossians chapter two verses 9-10 he also makes a strong link between fullness and Christ: 'For in Christ all the fullness of the Deity livs in bodily form, and you have been given fullness in Christ, who is head over every power and authority.'

Why do we say everything was in place? Well. **Consider the Jews first of all.** Their land was like a political football for most of their history. They were the prey of super-powers like Egypt or Syria or Assyria or Babylon, apart from brief periods in the time of David and Solomon, and in the later period of Jeroboam II in Israel and Uzziah in Judah. Their high priests were a flop – they were as worldly and power-seeking as any other group. Their Old Testament was a crib, in which the Christ-child was ready to be laid, to borrow the terminology of Martin Luther. Their people were either hungry for reality, waiting for the consummation of Israel in the advent of a king Messiah, or were longing for a superman Messiah who would whisk them away from planet earth to his heavenly kingdom. **Secondly, consider the Greeks.** They had a rich culture which ringed the Mediterranean world, due to the foresight and planning of Alexander the Great, and provided a great unifying cement socially. They also had a bankrupt philosophy, projected in popular mode in their decadent theatres, and exemplified in the awful poisoning of one of their best thinkers, Socrates. One of the Greeks' greatest contributions was their language, its classical form was simplified as the language of the people, koine Greek, the language in which almost all of the New Testament was written. It is almost impossible to overstate the importance of this in the spread of the Gospel around the Mediterranean by the apostles.

Thirdly, consider the Romans. They had total control through the Roman Army. Israel was one of the worst trouble spots in the Empire, the kind of posting soldiers dreaded. The Romans knew their grip had to be strong there, so one of their first tasks was to build the Fortress of Antonia, next to the Jewish Temple, and much bigger than the Temple. They also made the priests on Temple duty collect their vestments for service each day, just to humiliate them. A major by-product of the the Army's power throughout the Empire was the famous 'Pax Romana', the Roman peace, which meant that there was safety for the population around the Empire. Another spin-off was that a significant number of Roman soldiers were Christians, and took the Gospel with them on their postings, as far as the Danube, so that Tertullian (ca. AD 160-220), the great Christian apologist could write: 'tribesmen have bowed the knee to Christ who have not yet bowed the knee to Caesar.' There was open communication by sea (the Mediterranean was cleared of pirates), and land (the Romans built a magnificent

road network which covered around fifty thousand miles. (Many of these roads are still in use today).
They like the Greeks were weary of a corrupt religion, like the cult of Mithras with its weird initiation ceremonies and its mumbo-jumbo.

How can anyone deny the existence of a God who could so orchestrate international events and movements so that His Son's birth was the most perfect example of Divine timing?
I hope you can take all this in and move towards God in repentance and faith as a response.

In our previous section, we have marvelled in God's amazing Timing, acting at a time when the world needed Him most, and everything was in place. Now let's move the spotlight from **God's Timing,** to **God's Touch.** The pregnant phrase in the passage is in verse 4, 'God sent His Son'- four words of one syllable each! There is no need to complicate matters in order to make them seem important. The Bible is like the sea. When we used to go on holiday to Cullen in Banffshire, there was a lovely sheltered sandy spot down at the harbour, where the children could paddle in safety, but out at the end of the pier there were currents and depths that could drown a man. Similarly, the Bible has terms which are so clear and simple that a child could understand. The Lord Jesus summed up His mission in words that can be accurately summarised in words of one syllable – Luke chapter 19 verse 10: 'for the Son of Man came to seek and to save that which was lost.' In Philippians 1 verse 1, the apostle Paul summarises his Christian life in words of one syllable: 'For me to live is Christ and to die is gain.' Yet each of these sayings have wrapped up within them the depths of the mind of God. Conversely, the apostle's argument in the letter to the Romans can tax the greatest intellects on earth.
'God sent His Son.' **God's Touch** is seen in sending His Son as a baby to earth. Babies are naturally so weak and vulnerable. Paul says a curious thing in 1 Corinthians when he mentions that 'the weakness of God is stronger than men.' I wonder what you think about that phrase 'the weakness of God.' The power-

brokers of earth measure strength often in terms of military might, like the number of divisions of soldiers in their army, or how much capacity they have for manufacturing nuclear weapons. When Hitler and Mussolini tried to persuade Stalin about the advantages of including the Pope in their alliances. Stalin is reputed to have asked 'How many divisions has he?' Where men look to their imagined might, God looks for a man. They trust in the kalashnikov, but God trusts in the cradle, which in Moses' case, was made of bulrushes. At a time of great crisis, God called the child of a formerly childless mother, and Samuel was greatly used by God as the last of the judges, and the first of the prophets. For God, the sending of Jesus was a divine masterstroke. Augustine says: 'Only man owed the debt, only God could pay the debt, so for the debt of our sin to be paid, God had to become a man.'

FW Boreham spins a yarn about Roaring Camp, one of these mining communities that sprung up during the Yukon gold rush. The centre of activity at Roaring Camp each evening was the saloon, a dirty spit-and-sawdust kind of a place, reeking with tobacco smoke, where the prospectors gathered after a day panning or digging for gold. . One night someone noticed a bundle of newspapers in the corner of the saloon, and found that there was a baby wrapped in the newspapers! A hush came over the saloon, and Big Jake, who had been a carpenter, offered to make a rosewood cradle for the baby. Then Diamond Lil the saloon girl confessed her mother had taught her to crochet, and she made a beautiful shawl for the baby. When they saw the baby in her spotless shawl, lying in her rosewood cradle, they said they would have to clean up the saloon, and draught-proof it properly in case the baby caught a cold or an infection. The baby actually transformed Roaring Camp, and it was said throughout the camp that things had never been the same since the baby came. Which things are a parable of the coming of the Christ-child, whose transforming power and grace has become a reality in many a life, and during His earthly life He was a transforming influence for women and homeless and the sick and the ladies and the slaves and the outcasts, as well as a few people of wealth and status. 'In the fullness of time, God sent His Son...'

The text says in verse 4 that Jesus was 'born of a woman.' This was part of His self-emptying. Paul says in Philippians 2 verse 7: 'He made Himself nothing, taking the very nature of a servant, being made in human likeness.' In the careful language of Romans chapter 8 verse 3 'For what the law could not do in that it was weakened by the sinful nature, God did by sending His own Son in the likeness of sinful man ...' Jesus was the Son of Mary as well as the Son of God. He was fully human as well as fully divine.

Dr Alexander Whyte of Free St George's Edinburgh, a prince among preachers who was brought up in a two-roomed cottage in Kirriemuir, Angus, and whose sermons on 'Bible Characters' are still excellent, wrote this about Mary: 'On a thousand sacred canvases we are shown the angel of the Annunciation presenting Mary with a branch of a lily as an emblem of her beauty and as a seal of her purity. But why has no spiritual artist stained the whiteness of the lily with the red blood of a broken heart? ...Blessed among women as all the time she was; like the Passover lamb also she was set apart to be a divine sacrifice, and to have a sword thrust through her heart....We must give Mary her promised due. We must not allow ourselves to entertain a grudge against the mother of our Lord because some enthusiasts for her have given her more than her due. She magnified the Lord, and her spirit rejoiced in God her Saviour.'

Mary freely acknowledged God as her Saviour, because she was keenly aware of her needs as a sinner.

Jesus was also 'born under the law'. In John chapter 1 verse says 'He came to His own things', which probably indicates His own cultural and religious context, in the good providence of God. At His baptism at the River Jordan, God the Father expressed His verdict and pleasure on the hidden years from infancy, boyhood and twenties, by saying: This is my beloved Son in whom I am well pleased.' He lived in a good-sized, poor family in Nazareth, was subject to Mary and Joseph, attended synagogue and learned the skills of a carpenter without fuss. He had come to 'redeem those who were under the law', Professor AM Hunter says, 'that is, to buy us out of bondage to the law by enduring and exhausting in Himself the curse of the law (chapter 3 verse 13), moving from the obscurity of Nazareth to the awful limelight of the Cross.

During the First World War, (1914-1918) there was a story told of a middle class couple in England whose son was a subaltern, a first lieutenant, fighting in the trenches. He was wounded, and was rescued from no-man's-land by a brave private soldier, but unfortunately their son died.

After the War, the parents traced the infantryman, and invited him to their home. He arrived late, in a bedraggled state, the worse of drink. His language and table manners were appalling, and the parents said goodbye with some relief, and the wife said: 'did our son die for a wretch like that!'

The Lord Jesus Christ died for wretched sinners like us, becoming a curse in order to redeem us. Have you said 'thank you' yet?'

In verses 1-4, we have been looking at **God's Timing** in the sending of his Son. In verses 5-7, Paul marks out **God's Target** in all this, so that we might be Born Free as the redeemed, liberated sons and daughters of the living God. We become sons with rights in verse 5 sons with relationship in verse 6 and sons with receipts in verse 7. Verse 5 says that Jesus died to redeem us ....'that we might receive the full rights of sons.'

John 1 verse 12 says, 'to all those who received Him, to those who believed in His name, He gave the right to become children of God.' In the Graeco-Roman world, there was a legal device whereby a wealthy childless man could adopt a slave youth into his family, so that this penniless youth could cease to be a slave and become a son and heir. Now, there's a good 'rags to riches' story! Here is a better one. It's the same in Christian experience –slaves become sons and sons become heirs of God and co-heirs with Christ. (see Romans 8 verse 17.) This completes God's double work in our lives – redemption and adoption.

The Christian life is only possible through God taking up residence in each believer's life through the Holy Spirit. Romans 8 verse 9 says: 'You, however are controlled not by the sinful nature, but by the Spirit, if the Spirit of God lives in you. And if anyone does not have the Spirit of Christ, he does not belong to Christ.' One of the proofs of sonship is the heightened intimacy shown in addressing God as 'Abba, Father'. Paul helpfully provides a translation of the Aramaic diminutive word Abba, the word small boys used when speaking to their Daddy in the time of Paul, and the word which begins Luke's version of the Lord's Prayer. Like the word agape, which means love, Abba is one of those New Testament, new verbal coins minted on the lips of Christians, with the encouragement of the Lord Jesus, and the apostle Paul.

Therefore the indwelling Spirit gives this anointing, or unction (see 1 John 2 verse 20) which reassures of our sonship, and prompts us in our prayers, not in any pyrotechnic display, but in a quiet understanding that we belong to God.

QUESTIONS FOR DISCUSSION
4 v 1-11.

1. Is sinful living a form of slavery? Discuss.

2. See 4 v 4 . Is it important that Jesus' birth was a historical fact, or is the VALUE of His life and death more important?

3. What proof of real Christian experience have we in 4 v 6-7?

4. Discuss what factors can turn people back to live like they lived formerly.

CHAPTER 11.

PASTOR AND PEOPLE
Galatians chapter 4 verses 12-20.

We move on in our study to look at Galatians chapter 4 verses 12-20. It is the relationship between Paul and the Galatians, Pastor and People that is in focus in this section.

Let's hear part of it in the Message translation: 'My dear friends, what I would really like you to do is to try to put yourselves in my shoes to the same extent to the same extent that I, when I was with you, put myself in yours. You were very sensitive and kind then. You did not come down on me personally. You were well aware that that the reason I ended up preaching to you was that I was physically broken, and so, prevented from continuing my journey. I was forced to stop with you. That is how I came to preach to you.

And don't you remember that even though taking in a sick guest was most troublesome for you, you chose to treat me as well as you would have treated an angel of God – as well as you would have treated Jesus Himself if He had visited you! What has happened to the satisfaction you felt at that time? There were some of you who, if possible, would have given your very eyes to me – that is how deeply you cared! And now have I suddenly become your enemy simply by telling the truth? I can't believe it.'

It is obvious from Paul's letters that he related well to people wherever he went. This is especially clear here and in the Philippian letter, and most of all in the Thessalonian letters, when you consider that he was there for only about three weeks. The relationship between pastor and people is a special one, and Paul must have worked very hard to build good solid friendships. We can remember with profit the relationship between the Lord Jesus and His disciples. They answered His call, and shared His life, learned His ways and knew His mind. That is how Paul also walked with Jesus, spiritually.

We must also remember that he often worked as a tentmaker so that, although he had the right to expect financial and practical hospitality, people would not be able to accuse him justifiably of 'living off' the Christians he visited. He wrote in 1 Thessalonians 2 verses 5 and 9: 'You know we never used flattery, nor did we put on a mask to cover up greed – God is our witness....Surely you remember, brothers, our toil and hardship; we worked night and day in order not to be a burden to anyone while we preached the gospel of God to you.'

He wrote kindly to the Philippians in chapter 4 verses 13-16: 'Whatever I have, wherever I am, I can make it through anything in the One who makes me who I am. I don't mean that your help didn't mean a lot to me – it did. It was a beautiful thing that you came alongside me in my troubles. You Philippians well know, and you can be sure I will never forget it, that when I left the Macedonian churches...not one church helped in the give and take of the work – except you.'....

The pastor-and-people relationship is rather like a courtship between a boy and girl. There is the 'getting to know you, getting to know all about you' period. Then the relationship deepens and love and mutual respect develops as they get closer. It is an unusual relationship. I was involved in this kind of pastor-and-people relationships for over twenty years of my working life. The pastoral ministry is one of the few 'jobs' where you are loved by the people you work for, and paid for doing the thing you love doing most of all on this earth. The pastor is not paid a wage or a salary. The ministry is a calling, a vocation, not merely a job. The pastor or minister does not have an 'hourly rate', nor is it easy to figure out how many hours he works per week. He may be with a family late at night, or praying over a sick child's cot in a children's hospital in the middle of the night. He receives a stipend, which is a payment made for services rendered. Of course it is difficult to monitor the work he does, and sometimes there is no equivalent to a line manager, someone to whom he is answerable. Because he is in a position of trust, he does not have to submit a time sheet! Having said that, I know a church which tried to impose that on its minister! As part of my calling, I travelled all over Scotland to preach by invitation in many churches, and observed ministers at home and ministers at work. I served on committees interviewing candidates for ministry, and as moderator during about eight vacancies, which involved vetting profiles and interviewing ministers. The majority of pastors wear themselves out in the service of God and His people, often overworked and underpaid. I have been constantly amazed at the apparently endless patience exercised by their wives and families. Sadly, for various reasons, there are a few lazy bounders, frauds and phoneys in ministry, who do the minimum and function as taxi-drivers, child-minders, and message-boys, who wear their masks and distance themselves from their families and their flock. They are plastic people, who go about wearing their masks, and are unaware that ordinary folk can see right through them. Only Christians would put up with them. They could not hold down any job where their work is under scrutiny. Paul was not like that. These charlatans could not say what he said in Galatians 4 verse 12, ' I plead with you, brothers, become like me, for I became like you.' Imagine being able to look someone in the eye and say that! Admittedly the Greek text is rather jagged and ambiguous. There is only one verb 'Become as I, because I also as you, brothers...' The presence of the verb 'I plead' after this first clause is a significant watershed for the second part, or request section of the letter. The personal appeal here in verses 12-20 is followed by a Scriptural appeal in chapter 4 verses 21-31, and an authoritative appeal in chapter 5 verses 1-12, and an ethical appeal in chapter 5 verse 13 – chapter 6 verse 10.

Walter Hansen says the entire rebuke section of the letter, chapter 1 verse 6 – chapter 4 verse 11 establishes the background for this appeal. Paul had reacted to the false teachers by asserting his own calling by God and repudiation of any other message but the way to God by faith alone in Christ alone, full stop! They had allowed themselves to be confused and their thinking clouded by ideas that they needed something else by way of religious performance of ritual to qualify for God's blessing and God's salvation. In Acts chapter 26 verses 29, Paul says; 'Short time or long – I pray God that not only you but all who are listening to me today may become what I am, except for these chains.' Therefore he is probably meaning here in Galatians, that he wants them, having been born free in Christ to continue in that freedom as Paul had, without any spiritual chains to tie them down or hold them back in their Christian progress. He didn't want them to become Jews, he just wanted them to become like him – a child of God, born free. As he says in chapter 5 verse 1 'It is for freedom that Christ has set us free.' On reflection, how many of us could say to others 'become like me'. The imitation of Christ is an impossible ethic apart from grace and the indwelling Holy Spirit of God in human lives, so the quality of Paul's life must have been very high for him to write this. (see also 1 Corinthians chapter 4 verse 16. chapter 11 verse 1. Philippians chapter 3 verse 17 and chapter 4 verse 9).

In this chapter we're looking at Galatians chapter 4 verses 12-20 under the heading 'Pastor and People'. We've been saying that in verse 12 Paul was saying 'become like me' that is in his sense of being born free as God's child, ready to live by and share the Gospel of God's free and sovereign grace, through faith in Christ –full stop- without any additions, subtractions or multiplications. The apostle Paul also says in this verse 'I also as you, brothers', which I take to mean either 'I became as you are' or 'I have become as you are'. This tells us that when he came, he did not come condescendingly, like the man on the old Radio Show (was it Billy Cotton's Band Show?) 'Hey you down there, you with the glasses'. The true pastor should be the people's flexible friend, and identify with them. I cannot describe the look of horror on the face of a young minister who was asking how he could raise his church's profile in the district, and I suggested that he bought a bicycle, and cycled to visit his people! Very few people look at who is driving a car, but you get noticed on a bicycle, and can stop readily to talk to people. I know a young Baptist pastor who went to work in a Glasgow housing estate, and within the first week, some young vandal spray-painted a cross on the bonnet of his car when it was parked outside the church. 'Leave it', he said and drove around for a month. He said by the end of the month a lot of people knew who the Baptist pastor was! I paraphrased a section from an Alexander Maclaren sermon, where he said that you would never clean up the street by standing at the end of it with an aerosol can saying 'Be thou clean!' Maclaren said 'if you want to

clean up the street, you have to get involved with the filth.'
Jesus got involved with filth, touching lepers, inviting Himself to meals with tax-collectors and other low types, and so on. This is a wonderful principle for all ministry, evangelism and missionary work. It was a daring thing when the missionaries of the China Inland Mission started to wear Chinese-style clothes. In 1 Thessalonians 2 verse 7 Paul writes: '...we were gentle among you, like a mother caring for her little children.' Paul introduces on of the most intimate images in the world – a nursing mother breast-feeding her baby. For the baby to relax and feed, mother has to adapt her shape to the shape of the baby, to give a combined image of warmth and intimacy and unity. That is what Paul was like among the Philippians, or the Thessalonians, or here with the Galatian believers. 'Become as I, because I also as you, brothers...'

We're looking at Galatians 4 verses 12-20, and we've seen **Paul's appeal in verse 12.** From the latter part of verse 12 to verse 16, we see the **treatment the Galatians gave Paul.** 'You have done me no wrong.' He was worn out when he came to them. Sometimes the Lord's servants get tired! Sometimes they become stressed! There is a stress in the work which is bearable and appropriate. Clinical psychologists call it 'eu-stress' which is literally 'well stress', or 'good stress.' This is the kind of stress at which tuned violin strings produce the solo parts in the beautiful Mendelssohn violin concerto, for example. Then there is 'distress' which is unbearable and inappropriate, and the strings as it were, snap.

Paul's illness had been a sore trial for the Galatians but they had treated him with lots of t.l.c. (tender loving care). His illness was obvious and certainly the kind that could be offensive to an audience. Paul suffered from some physical problem. He introduces it in 2nd Corinthians chapter 12 verse 7 as a counterweight to the top-grade, inexpressible revelations God had given him 'To keep me from becoming conceited because of these surpassingly great revelations, there was given me a thorn in my flesh, a messenger of Satan, to torment me.' He does not directly state that God gave this to him, for God is not the subject of the verb, and he goes on to say that after three instances of pleading with God to remove it, God reassured him that His grace was sufficient for him, and that God's strength was perfected in weakness. Much ink has been spilt discussing what Paul's thorn in the flesh was. Passing on from the flippant suggestion that it was his wife (we don't think he had one), some have suggested it was some recurrent physical problem, like malaria (Pamphylia and the coastal plain in that area were rife with malarial fever), or epilepsy (which could be very demeaning for a preacher, hence 2 Corinthians 10 verse 10 A.V.'his bodily presence is weak'). This passage in Galatians - especially chapter 4 verse 15: 'I can testify that, if you could have done so, you would have torn out your eyes and given them to me'- would indicate some eye disease like trachoma. The physically repulsive aspect of his 'thorn' is hinted at in verse 14 'you did not treat me with contempt or scorn' The verb translated 'treat with...scorn' is an onomatopaeic (it sounds like it means,'ekptuo=to spit out') means 'you did not spit (me) out'. They were sensitive to his needs, and cared for him as if he were an angel visiting them, or even the Lord Jesus Christ! The idea of receiving a visitor as if he were Jesus Christ is probably connected with the role of apostles, who were after all personal representatives, and receiving such a person was equivalent to receiving the sender. (see Matthew chapter 10 verses 40-42).

This is a beautiful passage reflecting the help that Christians can be to a suffering fellow-Christian. I once knew a young couple who attended a tent mission conducted by a visiting evangelist at the invitation of a neighbouring church. The evangelist had just returned to work after six weeks off through stress, so he was fragile to say the least. The young couple were horrified to hear that, although the inviting church had lots of available hospitality in members' homes, they had put the evangelist on a camp bed in the toilet of their church hall. The couple used to 'smuggle' him home for meals and a decent bed, and the wife did his washing, which was no little task, because he was continually scratching, and his shirts were blood-stained! A life-long friendship developed between the couple and the evangelist. They behaved towards him as the Galatians behaved towards Paul. Hospitality is a precious gift. Sometimes we take in angels unawares!

We're looking at Galatians chapter 4 verses 12-20, under the heading Pastor and people, and we've seen the lovely welcome the Galatians gave to Paul, one of the Lord's worn-out tools. I have lots of stories to tell about hospitality, having been 'on the road' sometimes as a preacher. I remember taking part in a pulpit exchange and being given hospitality in a big stone-built Victorian manse which seemed as cold as the grave. The retired minister and his wife who lived in it gave me a meagre meal of watery mince, a scrape of potatoes and a few peas. They were obviously living in poverty, but as I left he had a few books to give me that he thought would help the young preacher. What a contrast between the warmth of their welcome and the bleakness of their physical circumstances!
Paul is astounded that a friendship which developed out of his physical need and dependency is going to be scrapped by them because he gave them the gospel straight from the shoulder.
In verses 17 and 18 Paul questions their motives, pointing out that their keen and plausible approach had a selfish motive to win followers of themselves rather than followers of Christ. He doesn't want to devalue zeal, but it must be driving them for a good purpose, rather than providing an ego massage for the false teachers. He wanted them to stand for Christ even when Paul was not there. Good school teachers work for the day when their classroom discipline has become internalised in the children's minds, so that the children get on with their work, even when the teacher is not leaning over their shoulder. Paul says 'not just when I am with you'. This leads him into an impassioned statement which reflects his longings about them. Here it is in Professor Lorimer's translation of the New Testament in Scots : 'My bairnies – weill may I sae caa ye, for I am aince mair in sair grip wi' ye, or Christ be formed ithin ye. Oh, gin I wis amang ye eenou, an coud speak anither gate til ye, for I am fair fickelt about ye!' Although this is a good example of an emotional appeal in Paul, his appeals could be reasoned and complex (see chapter 3 verse 6 – chapter 4 verse 7). He compares himself here like a mother in the travails of childbirth, and sees the end product as Christ being formed in them, 'until you take the

shape of Christ'. He uses the same form of sharing- the- shape imagery in Philippians chapter 3 verse 10 'becoming like Him in His death.'

Paul becomes intensely personal in this section, which encourages us to think that the emotional parts of Scripture have to be taken seriously. We should not read the Bible in public as if we were reading the telephone directory, but we should read to give the sense, including the sections where the writer seems to be wearing his heart on his sleeve. The Bible has a broader appeal than being a book for academics, and the preaching and teaching of its message can be given with passion and conviction. John Bunyan said about his preaching method : 'I preached what I did feel, what I smartingly did feel.'

Scot McKnight raises an interesting question in connection with Paul's appeal in this passage. Is there a difference between an apostle and a pastor nurturing others, and says: 'an apostle has a kind of authority that neither a pastor nor a parent nor a 'discipler' dare to think they have. Paul's goal and ours is to see Christ formed in others. There is a divine balance between them becoming like him, and him becoming like them.'
Another point from the passage is that a repulsive illness can be an impediment to communication, but the Holy Spirit of God can overcome natural barriers. Paul's thorn was repulsive, but Galatians came to Christ. Your present author is not silver-tongued nor golden-voiced. He is neither tall, blonde nor American. The Scottish preacher Thomas Guthrie said 'When you receive a wonderful message from a divine source, please do not complain about the quality of the paper!' Tonight, God could set you alight as a result of this letter. You could repudiate any false teaching which has spellbound you, and you could cling to Christ and His gospel of grace. He could be formed in you, and you could go on and serve Him for the rest of your life. That is my prayer and hope for you. God bless you.

QUESTIONS FOR DISCUSSION
4 v 12-20

1. 'Become like me, for I became like you.' (verse 12) Discuss ways in which we can get alongside Christian brothers and sisters.

2. See verse 14. How could someone else's illness be a trial for us? Exchange ideas about what Paul's illness might be.

3. What was wrong with the zeal of the false teachers?

4. Discuss Paul's agonies as a pastor in relation to his people.

Chapter 12

WHAT USE IS THE OLD TESTAMENT?
Galatians 4 verses 21 – 31.

In this chapter, we are looking at Galatians chapter 4 verses 21 to 31, which is possibly the most obscure and difficult section in this letter. We have to face up to the difficult bits of the Bible as well as the straightforward bits. Having argued for freedom from chapter 1 and verse 1 of the letter, and having tried to present his case personally for being born free into God's family by faith alone through grace alone, Paul takes on the false teachers in their own style of argument, which copied the rabbis, and shows how freedom figures in two covenants, two women, two children and two states. Now I realise some of you may be unfamiliar with the Old Testament, which Martin Luther regarded as the crib in which the Christ-child is laid. Being a New Testament Christian instead of a Bible Christian is a bit like breathing with only one lung, or rowing in circles with only one oar. What is latent in the Old Testament becomes patent in the New Testament. The Bible contains one dispensation of grace under two covenants, the Old and New Testaments. The whole Bible package can be reviewed in three phrases: The King will Come (Old Testament), The King has Come (Gospels/Acts/ New Testament letters), and a golden thread running through both Testaments would be The King Will Come Again. Bishop Taylor-Smith had three different phrases to sum up the Bible: The first one was : God is (that is, He exists). The second one was : God is Love. And the third one is: God Loves Me. If I were choosing an over-arching, summary theme for the Old Testament it would be Righteousness – Righteousness given (in Creation) / Righteousness Lost (in the Fall) / Righteousness Promised (through Abraham) /Righteousness Regulated by Law/ Righteousness Fought for (in the historical books) Righteousness Set to Music (in Psalms) Righteousness Debated (in the Wisdom Books) and Righteousness Predicted (in the Books of the Prophets).

As we said earlier, Paul in this passage adopts the mantle of the rabbis, so beloved by his opponents the false teachers, and argues the way they argued in order to show from Scripture God's emphasis on freedom. In Ian Murray's account of revival in Australia, he tells about an evangelist who had a burden for the tough, far-travelled sheep-shearers. The evangelist went to where they were, (like Paul did with the Galatians). He talked with them and tried to obtain opportunities to preach the Gospel among them. The leader of one group of these nasties told the evangelist the only way he could preach to them was to fight their best fighter in the boxing ring. He insisted on this as a pre-condition, but he did not know that the evangelist was a converted prize-fighter! The match was set up, the evangelist quickly decked their best fighter. Their champion became a horizontal champion, and the evangelist got a very respectful hearing...

In this section Paul takes on the Lovers of Jewish Law on their own ground, or their 'ain kail yerd' as the Scots would say, arguing the way the rabbis argued except he argues to prove that God had planned to replace the Old Covenant of Sinai by a New Covenant of Freedom. This is Paul's Scriptural appeal, following his personal appeal 'become like me' (verse 12).

Scholars debate whether Paul was treating this Old Testament passage as allegory or typology. Now some of us wouldn't recognise allegory or typology if we saw them in our porridge, so perhaps we should try to find out what they are. My English teacher used to say that a men's best friend is his dictionary, so here goes : **Allegory** occurs in a story, play or poem in the form of symbols which can be unearthed from underlying truths. **Typology** is the use of prototype ideas and their development in later fulfilment of God's plan of salvation history. Technically, students talk about the Old Testament **type** and the New Testament **antitype.** Some prefer the term **homology** instead of **typology,** where we look for an exact correspondence between the Old Testament 'type' and its New Testament 'antitype'. If you ever did geometry at school, it's like similar triangles. When you are studying similar triangles, the existence of three sides is not the measure of correspondence, but there has to be an exact ratio between all of the three sides. In organic chemistry, there are series of compounds like the paraffin hydrocarbons – for example, ethane, methane propane and butane- where there is an exact difference between each member in the series.

To take a Biblical example, in Exodus chapter 12 there is the story of the Passover, and in one of his Corinthian letters Paul talks about 'Christ our Passover' is sacrificed for us. There is a direct link between the Old and New Testament images. In Numbers chapter 21 in the Old Testament, there is a cameo incident where the people of Israel were being bitten by snakes, and they asked Moses to intercede with God on their behalf. Moses gave the solution ; they had to make a bronze snake and put it on a pole in the centre of their camp. Everyone who looked, were healed. Is this the end of the story? Don't you believe it! In John chapter 3 in the New Testament, the incident takes 'centre stage' in the teaching of Jesus. One of the difficulties is recognising the beginning from the end! Who would have guessed that the beginning of the oak tree was the acorn!

One thing is certain – Paul spent time with God after his conversion. He was in Arabia for about three years, and his view of the Jewish Scriptures was revolutionised. The conclusion drawn is that Paul combines both techniques in his use of these Old Testament passages.

Now, let's get into chapter 4 verses 21-26, which was best summarised by Professor Archibald Hunter of Aberdeen. I agree with the verdict of the Dictionary of Scottish History and Theology on him: 'a writer of exceptional clarity.' He wrote: ' Abraham had two sons: Ishmael, the son of the slave-woman Hagar, was born in the ordinary course of nature; and Isaac, son of the free-woman Sarah, was born following a divine promise when Sarah seemed too old to have a family.

Now, Paul explains, there is a deep meaning in this story. The two women with their sons symbolise two covenants, or dispensations. Hagar, mother of the despised Ishmaelites, represents the Sinai Covenant, as her outcast children represent the Jews in bondage to the law. Sarah, however, represents the New Covenant, and her children are the men of faith, Jew and

Gentile, who live for freedom. This is the meaning of verses 21-26, in which Paul's aim is to show from Scripture that God planned to replace the Law and the Old Covenant of Sinai by a New Covenant of Freedom.'

If the Galatians want to be live under the rule of Jewish law, Paul asks in verse 21 whether they are fully aware of what the law says to them. In chapter 4 verse 10, some are already trying to follow the Jewish calendar. In chapter 5 verse 2, we read that some of them have been circumcised. In chapter 5 verse 3, he points out that a circumcised person must keep the whole law. In the section we are looking at in chapter 4, he is saying that of they want to go the law route, here's how it applies in your situation. Then he launches into a passage which would trouble a Philadelphia lawyer, never mind a Galatian convert! He defends his position somewhat in verse 24 by saying that 'these things may be taken figuratively.' His real aim is to identify the Galatian Christians as the true children of Abraham, the children of the free woman, and the children of promise. This had been his argument in chapter 3 verse 29, where they were sons of Abraham and heirs of the promise God gave Abraham.

Paul begins with a glance at Abraham's faith in chapter 3 verse 6-14, at covenants chapter 3 verses 15-25, and at sonship from chapter 3 verse 26 to chapter 4 verse 20. In the final argument, Paul is drawing two divergent lines: Abraham-Sarah-Isaac and Abraham-Hagar-Ishmael. Apparently, it was part of the teaching style of the Jewish rabbis to finish with a flourish, by using some allegory/type to drive home the points he had been making in his main speech or lesson. The device was regularly used by people like Philo of Alexandria (c20BC – c AD 50), a Jewish thinker and scholar.

In Galatians chapter 3 verse 21, Paul is inviting his opponents into the ring, as it were, pointing out the implications of their trust in the law. In verse 22 and 23 he is eliciting the Jewish trust in Abraham as the Father of the Jewish race. John the Baptist assumed the same when he spoke by the River Jordan: 'Do not presume to say to yourselves, 'we have Abraham as our father. (Matthew chapter 3 verse 9). This was their claim to Jesus 'We are descendants of Abraham, and have never been in bondage to anyone.' In verses 22 and 23, Paul lifts his argument to a higher plane – Being part of Abraham's line is not a matter of being registered, like a pedigree dog registered with the Kennel Club, but a matter of believing and obeying in the good old Abraham way, believing in the same God who brought life from the dead in the case of Isaac's birth to Sarah, or in the case of Jesus rising from the tomb. Isaac and Ishmael were both Abraham's sons, but they had different mothers. Abraham was working within the legal framework of his time by treating Hagar as his wife. According to Nuzi (Mesopotamian) law, a childless wife was responsible for providing a substitute. However, if the first wife later produced a child, her child assumed first place in inheritance any children the 'substitute' had. Since the social status of the mothers determined the social status of their sons, Ishmael was a slave and Isaac was free. Walter Hansen points out that there was nothing supernatural about Ishmael's birth – it happened 'in the ordinary way', a good NIV equivalent of 'according to the flesh', which avoids any judgemental overtones regarding the term 'flesh'. On the other hand, the only way that Abraham's sexual union with his aged, barren wife Sarah could have resulted in conception was by divine intervention to fulfil God's promise.

The apostle Paul is arguing that God's covenant of freedom, which goes back to Abraham, far earlier than Moses, is of a distinctively superior quality, especially when we investigate the family links to the two covenants. In Galatians 4 verses 21-23, he stays with the factual Biblical content of the Genesis narratives. In Galatians 4 verses 24-26, he dons his seven-league boots, so to speak, and legs it into a series of symbolic comparisons which exemplify spiritual truths. Abraham in his own life exemplifies the only two possible attitudes towards God – faith and unbelief. This is central and basic. The Jewish objector or false teacher would not accept the new covenant as something now in force. He would believe it could not have come into being without his noticing it. Paul presses home this difference. Paul had argued earlier in the letter that law-keeping as a way to salvation led only into bondage. Therefore the Sinai covenant 'bears sons destined to become slaves.' The Jews were

'Abraham's seed' and children of the covenant with Abraham as truly as they were children of the covenant with Moses. But as long as they looked on the law and its performance as a possible means of salvation, such slavery was inevitable. This was a hammer-blow to Jewish or false teacher's pride. It bore down on them like a panzer division, because they thought of themselves as Isaac's offspring, not part of the 'Ishmaelites', those 'wild-donkey', desert-dwellers of the Negev. Paul's argument carried on the main line Sarah-Isaac-Mount Zion-heavenly Jerusalem-freedom-Paul-New Covenant line. His argument shunts the false teachers on to the Hagar-Ishmael-Mount Sinai-earthly Jerusalem-slavery-Judaisers-Old Covenant line! Scot McKnight writes: 'Paul is saying that those who believe in Christ are living in the new era, the era of fulfilment.' One of the great Jewish phrases of anticipation was 'days are coming'. Remember how Jesus kept saying 'my hour has not yet come,' and then how He responded to the Greeks who wanted to see Him at the Feast of the Passover in Jerusalem 'the hour has come for the Son of Man to be glorified. I tell you the truth, unless a grain of wheat falls into the ground and dies, it remains only a single seed. But if it dies, it produces many seeds.' (John 12 verses 23-24).

Having looked at the textual basis from the Genesis narratives in the Old Testament in verses 21-23, and then set out some symbolical spin-offs in verses 24-27, Paul ties up the loose ends in verses 28-30, and nails down his application. This brings us back to the main theme in this theological symphony – 'Born free' In verses 28-30, he tells the Galatian Christians that 'they, like Isaac, are children of promise.' He alludes in verse 29 to Ishmael persecuting Isaac. There is no hard Biblical evidence for this, unless we press Genesis 21 verse 9 where it refers to Ishmael 'mocking', or 'teasing' or 'playing with' Isaac. In verse 29, where Paul says 'it is the same now', he may be referring to the perennial conflict between Arabs and Jews, linking in Ishmael as representative head of the Arabs. In the Genesis narrative, Abraham and Sarah broke Nuzi law by expelling Hagar. Slave women who had served as wives were to be well-treated, even when they had forfeited their inheritance rights. Nevertheless, Paul uses her expulsion to urge the Galatian Christians to repudiate the false teachers' insistence on following the 'Hagar' route to getting right with God. They are wrong to insist that the law must be adopted to become 'a son of Sarah.' They were emancipated permanently from that kind of slavery. They were 'Born Free', and should go on to savour their new-found freedom!

The themes of freedom and law in this passage, and throughout the letter raise the whole question of the role of law in Christian living. Have the Ten Commandments any relevance to our lives today? Many Christians think that the law has no valid claim or place in our Christian living. They would say that people who trust Christ are set free from any obligation to keep God's law. There was an old Sankey Hymn which said : 'Free from the law, O happy condition...'

Another school of thought is that Christians are set free to keep the law of God. They say that while law-keeping is out as a means of gaining salvation, Jesus validated the moral law of God, and made it permanently binding for lifestyle, but not for salvation Salvation is through faith alone, by grace alone, but the law is still a good part of God's help for us.. In the Sermon on the Mount, Jesus said He hadn't come to dispense with the law, but to fulfil it to the finest detail. Matthew chapter 5 verses 17-18 say: 'Do not think that I have come to abolish the Law or the Prophets; I have not come to abolish them, but to fulfil them. I tell you the truth, until heaven and earth disappear, not the smallest letter, not the least stroke of a pen, will by any means disappear from the Law, until everything is accomplished.' In the Letter to the Romans, the apostle Paul argues in chapter 7 that the law is 'holy, righteous and good' in verse 12, and 'spiritual' verse 14. The law is like a mirror, showing us that we are dirty and need cleansing. Another old analogy used by writers of the Puritan period, which fits Romans 7 very well is that the Law is like a sweeping brush, which has a good purpose, but may have the harmful side effect of stirring up sin. One of my friends used to say that 'No Smoking' signs made him want to smoke! He always was a rebel!
Puritan Christians used to say that God's Holy Spirit is given to

us to effect evangelical obedience. The great chapter on 'Life in the Spirit' is Romans chapter 8, and here's what Paul wrote in verses 3 and 4 : 'For what the Law was powerless to do in that it was weakened by the sinful nature, God did by sending His own Son in the likeness of sinful man, to be a sin offering. And so He condemned sin in sinful man, **in order that the righteous requirements of the Law might be fully met in us,** who do not live according to the sinful nature, but according to the Spirit.' The Ten Commandments are still useful, not least in defining holy conduct and exposing sinful behaviour. Paul seems to be arguing that the Holy Spirit enables Christians to live a holy life which pleases God and fulfils His Law. This fills out the Galatian picture a little...

It is inevitable that to become a Christian is to face some friction, or resistance, or positive persecution. How should we react to others around us who do not treat us well? In the film 'The Untouchables', Eliot Ness learns from the policeman Malone what the Chicago Way is with enemies like Al Capone – 'he brings a knife, you bring a gun; he lands one of yours in the hospital, you land one of his in the morgue.' The Glasgow Way was epitomised in the car sticker 'You toucha my car, I smasha your face.' The Jewish Way in the time of Jesus was 'Love your Jewish Neighbour and Hate your Gentile Enemy.' The Jesus Way can be defined as : 'Love God, Love your Neighbour, and Love your Enemies'. This is an impossible ethic apart from the grace of God, and the indwelling Spirit of God, because the natural reaction to any kind of opposition is to retaliate.

QUESTIONS FOR DISCUSSION
4 v 21-21

1.   Discuss the culture and problems of polygamy between Abraham and the ladies in his life.

2.   How does Paul explain the covenant of freedom from Chapter 4 v 24 onwards?

3.   'Christians are happy pilgrims rather than happy wanderers'. Discuss.

4.   'It is better to be a Bible Christian rather than a New Testament Christian.' Discuss.

OUTLINE OF GALATIANS CHAPTER 5.

Paul reminds the Galatians that freedom is the key result of Christ's work for them. Circumcision would be a retreat and return to the old bondage. Law-keeping as a way of being put right with God makes Christ's sacrifice valueless, and leads to spiritual alienation and decline. Faith expressed in love is God's way. Their progress has been halted, like a runner being impeded, or a batch of dough being spoiled by interference. Emasculation rather than circumcision would be better suited to Paul's persecutors!

Christian freedom must not be exploited in order to be destructively critical, but must express itself in practical love. The safe way through their conflicts is to avoid sinful practices by living in the power of the Spirit. People who display different manifestations of their sinful nature will forfeit God's blessing and kingly rule.

The lovely, balanced and ethical harvest of the Spirit will characterise those who crucify the sinful nature, and live and march in step with the Holy Spirit.

CHAPTER 13.

FALSE AND TRUE RELIGION
Galatians Chapter 5 verses 1- 15.

In this section of the letter, we are looking at Galatians chapter 5 verses 1 to 15 under the heading 'False and True Religion'. Paul had digressed in the latter part of chapter 4 to use the Old Testament to prove the priority of faith and promise over performance and law.

I used to attend our local cinemas when I was young, and we were used to seeing two films per show, the 'A' picture and the 'B' picture. We used to refer to the 'A' picture as 'the big picture', and here in Galatians 5 verse 1, Paul called his readers at Galatia back to the big picture: 'It is for **freedom** that Christ has us free. Stand firm then, and do not let yourselves be burdened again by a yoke of slavery.' Let's repeat this verse in the Message translation, and continue on a bit: **'Christ has set us free to live a free life.** So take your stand! Never again let anyone put a harness of slavery on you.

I am emphatic about this. The moment any of you submits to circumcision or any other rule-keeping system, at that moment Christ's hard-won gift of freedom is squandered. I repeat my warning: the person who accepts the ways of circumcision trades all the advantages of the free life in Christ for the obligations of the slave life of the law. I suspect you would never intend this, but this is what happens. When we attempt to live by our own religious plans and projects, we are cut off from grace, you fall out of grace. Meanwhile we expectantly wait for a satisfying relationship with the Spirit. For in Christ, neither our most conscientious religion,nor disregard of religion, amounts to anything. What matters is something far more interior : faith expressed in love.'

The section from verses 2-15 can be divided into three parts, and within each part there is a contrast between false religion and true religion. The text oscillates back and forward like a weaver's shuttle between the false and the true...**The three sections are : verses 2-6, verses 7-12, and verses 13-15.** False religion is like whitewash, just an exterior covering, or like a weed spreading in the garden, intrinsically useless, and inhibiting the growth of good healthy plants. Verses 2-6 deal with the false religion associated with circumcision, which leads to bondage and alienation from God. It is like a slave losing his liberty. The problem is that the procedure involved the Galatian Christians in the whole package of a dependency culture where everyone involved in it is a prisoner of the system. In verses 2-6, it is like debtor losing his wealth. We are able easily to identify features of our secular culture with this, like drug or alcohol dependency, but here the application Paul makes is religious, and is in fact more potentially dangerous or even lethal. He says it devalues Christ, puts Him at a lower level than a medical/theological procedure, and alienates Him from the person who has been circumcised (verse 3-4). Although circumcision was practised widely among the nations of the Fertile Crescent in the Middle East, to the Jews the rite was a special sign of their separation to God. The Jews regarded themselves as especially enriched in their heritage. **In verses 5-6,** Paul highlights the expectations of the true believer. Christians also are especially enriched in Christ. In 2 Corinthians 8 verse 9 Paul writes: 'For you know the grace of our Lord Jesus Christ, that though He was rich, yet for your sakes He became poor so that you through His poverty might become rich.'

The Holy Spirit's real presence in the life of a believer heightens his belief that the righteousness he received would be a reality which lasted not only for this life, but also beyond death. The realisation of this expectation involves both vindication and final victory.

Isn't that a great message of hope for so many people today whose circumstances would drive them out of their heads with despair?!

In verses 7-12, we see a damaging interruption and a damaging influence. If verse 1 can be applied to a slave losing his freedom, and verses 2-6 can be applied to a debtor losing his wealth, then verses 7-12 can be compared to a runner losing his direction.

The New Testament writings, and Paul's letters in particular, use lots of athletic imagery. (The people of the New Testament period were familiar with the Olympic Games and the Isthmian Games.) The Letter to the Hebrews talks about running with perseverance the race that is set before us, surrounded by a great cloud of witnesses, like spectators, and as we run, fixing our eyes on Jesus the Pioneer and Perfecter of our faith. (Hebrews 12 verses 1-2). Paul reviews his life as having finished the race, and kept the faith, and having a crown of righteousness waiting for him (2 Timothy 4 verses 7 and 8).   Paul writes at length about the Christian faith in the imagery of running and boxing in 1 Corinthians chapter 9 verses 24-27 : 'Do you not know that in a race all the runners run, but only one gets the prize? Run in such a way as to get the prize. Everyone who competes in the Games goes into strict training. They do it to gain a crown that will not last; but we do it to get a crown that will last for ever. Therefore I do not run like a man running aimlessly; I do not fight like a man beating the air. No, I beat my body and make it my slave so that after I have preached to others, I myself will not be disqualified for the prize'. In our Galatians passage, he alludes to something any spectator is familiar with – runners cutting in on other runners. The Message translates chapter 5 verse 7 forwards like this: 'You were running superbly! Who cut in on you, deflecting you from the true course of obedience. This detour doesn't come from the One who called you into the race in the first place.' In the imagery of Paul, the runners who 'cut in' were definitely the Judaising false teachers. It is tragically easy to be deflected from the path of God's will for our lives. Robert Frost, the American poet, in his poem about the woods in winter, writes;

'The woods are lovely, and very deep,
But I have many promises to keep,
And many miles to go before I sleep.'

Too many have responded to the allure of the woods. Paul does not want the Galatians to be side-tracked like this...

The damaging interruption of their Christian progress sprung from the damaging influence of the false teachers. In verse 9 Paul changes his imagery from running to baking, saying that 'a little yeast works through the whole batch of dough.' Some scholars think that yeast is a word picture of evil in Scripture, as it is here, but overall the stress may be on secret, silent, pervasive influence rather than evil activity. False teaching here will inevitably spread throughout the gathered fellowship of believers, like yeast in a batch of dough. In chapter 5 verse 12 Paul writes in a way which seems harsh and crude, but we have to view it in its cultural context. It would have been a sensational visual display if the male members of the Galatian churches had been circumcised by the false teachers. But if they want to put on a really sensational show, why not go the whole hog and emasculate themselves ! In Paul's time, the priests of Cybele, the mother goddess of the earth, castrated themselves with ritual pincers and placed their testicles in a box! The followers of the cult of Attis in Rome and Phrygia did likewise. Here Paul is willing to discredit circumcision by ranking it with the debased rituals of paganism...

I have pointed out that each section in this passage has two emphases. The true religion side of the coin here consists of the reference in verse 8 to their **godly call,** and more particularly to the One who called them, the Lord Jesus Christ. Secondly, the true religion emphasis finds an echo in verse 10 in their **godly confidence,** where Paul expresses his confident view that they will stay 'on course'. Thirdly, the true religion aspect is found in the **godly cross** mentioned in verse 11, where Paul says that involvement in promoting circumcision would effectively remove the offence of Christ's cross and suffering from the equation.

In the final section, **verses 13-15,** he warns them in the false religious department, not to abuse their call to freedom by indulging their sinful nature. John Stott says 'Christian freedom is freedom **FROM** sin, not freedom **TO** sin.' We inherited this fallen human nature from our parents, as they did from our grandparents.

Our fallen nature is warped, self-centred and weak, so that we are liable to fall before the slightest temptation.   He is not specific about how this can be done : 'But do not use your freedom to indulge the sinful nature.' People sometimes quote Augustine, who is supposed to have said 'Love God and do what you like!' I don't think that sits or fits with our text here. In Titus 2 verses 11 and 12, Paul writes 'For the grace of God... teaches us to say 'No' to ungodliness and worldly passion...' There is a negative aspect to godliness (which is of course an abbreviation of 'godlikeness'), as there is to most things in life that are worthwhile. When Bill Shankly was manager of Liverpool Football Club, he wouldn't sign players who smoked. He kept a close scrutiny of their drinking habits, and banned card-playing for money when travelling to away games. In the field of athletics there is a dimension called 'the loneliness of the long-distance runner'. Ordinary people training for marathon races have to train for at least 35 miles a week, which deprives them of some home comforts, out running in the rain and the cold. Indulging the sinful nature would cover things like our eating habits as well as sexual over-indulgence. In the second part of verse 13, Paul sets out a Christian recipe for the good life: 'rather, serve one another in love,' that is our freedom has to be expressed in service. This carries into the summary of the entire law in verse 14, 'love you neighbour as yourself', that is, our freedom has to be expressed in love as well as service. John Stott writes: 'Indeed, so far from having liberty to ignore, neglect or abuse our fellow-men, we are commanded to love them, and through love to serve them. We are not to use them as if they were things to serve us; we are to respect them as persons and give ourselves to serve them.' William Neill says: 'we are not to be one master with a lot of slaves, but each to be one poor slave with a lot of masters.'

The final part of this section reverses the order and we get the false religion section last instead of first. Paul writes 'If you keep on biting and devouring one another, watch out or you will be destroyed by each other.' Bitter tongues are an awful abuse of fellowship. It is possible to be 'done to death by slanderous tongues', as Dryden puts it. There is nothing more corrosive, damaging, confidence-sapping, and soul-destroying than rumour-mongering with a critical tongue. English literature's masterpiece on this theme is of course Shakespeare's play Othello, in which the insidious work of Iago led Othello on to destruction. In Act 3 Scene 3, Iago shows his awareness of the issues: 'Who steals my purse, steals trash – 'tis something, nothing; 'Twas mine, 'tis his, and has been slave to thousands; but he that filches from me my good name robs me of that which not enriches him, and makes me poor indeed.' Part of the problem of our sinful nature is that it precipitates quarrels and unhealthy arguments, name-calling and stereotyping.

The Galatian Christians exhibited the same capacity which is sadly found widely – the ability to argue about anything. This has dated from the time 'Tweedledum and Tweedledee set out to have a battle, for Tweedledum said Tweedledee had stole his nice new rattle', and is probably as old as the Garden of Eden.

Our gruesome talent for warfare was described in the pungent prose of Jonathan Swift in 'Gulliver's Travels', where Gulliver explained to his master in the Land of the Houyhnhnms the usual causes or motives that make one country go to war with another. Gulliver says:

'Differences in opinions hath cost many millions of lives – for instance, whether flesh be bread or bread be flesh, whether the juice of a certain berry be blood or wine...whether it be better to kiss a post or throw it in the fire; what is the best colour for a coat – whether black, white, red or grey.... Sometimes our neighbours want the things which we have, or have the things which we want, and we both fight till they take ours or give us theirs. It is a very justifiable cause of war to invade a country after the people have been wasted by famine, destroyed by pestilence, or embroiled by factions among themselves.... And to set forth the valour of my own dear countrymen I assured him that I had seen them blow up a hundred enemies at once, in a siege, and as many in a ship, and beheld the dead bodies come down in pieces from the clouds, to the great diversion of the spectators.'

In a recent television series, called 'The Neighbours from Hell', the broadcasters drew from a wealth of documentary evidence, illustrating our inexhaustible talent for not getting on with other people.

As I have said before, in my painful experience, churches can argue about the colour of paint, the number of rings on a church kitchen cooker, whether deacons should wear name tags, how much to pay a visiting music group, or whether a lady with a bunion should be allowed to wear a slipper instead of a shoe to come to church! Sometimes there are quarrels about Calvinism and Arminianism, charismatic versus non-charismatic worship styles, the role of women/children/senior citizens in church, inter-tribal quarrels about which families should be in leadership positions, or whether to have alcoholic or non-alcoholic communion wine.

People can snap at each other like pariah dogs, the scavengers of the streets, in a grim battle which involves a lot of biting (and back- biting), which is possibly the imagery of Paul's warning here about biting and devouring one another, and destroying one another. When churches descend to this, the community around certainly gets the message – 'don't go near that place! If that's Christianity, I want nothing to do with it!'

By way of contrast, Paul writes about the value of the grace of God in Titus 2 verse 12 : 'It teaches us to say 'no' to ungodliness and worldly passions , and to live self-controlled, upright and godly lives in this present age.' We are to live self-controlled lives as far as we are concerned, upright lives as far as those we come into contact with are concerned, and godly lives as far as God is concerned – which gives our Christian lives an internal, and external and an eternal dimension!

This section puts a lot of things in perspective for us. Let us close this chapter with John Stott's summing up of the section. 'This passage tells us at the outset that we are 'called to freedom', the freedom which is peace with God, the cleansing of our guilty conscience through faith in Christ crucified, the unutterable joy of forgiveness, acceptance, access and sonship, the experience of mercy without merit.

It goes on to describe how this liberty from systems of merit expresses itself in our duty to ourselves, our neighbour, and our God. It is freedom not to indulge the flesh but to control the flesh; freedom not to exploit our neighbour, but to serve our neighbour; freedom not to disregard the law, but to fulfil the law. Everyone who has been truly set free by Jesus Christ expresses his liberty in these three ways, first in self-control, next in loving service of his neighbour, and thirdly in obedience to the law of his God.

This is the freedom with which 'Christ has set us free'(verse 1), and to which we 'were called (verse 13). We are to stand firm in it, neither relapsing into slavery on the one hand, nor falling into licence on the other.'

QUESTIONS FOR DISCUSSION
5 v 1-15

1. How would you relate and explain the words law, grace, faith and love?

2. Discuss the best/worst ways of using our Christian freedom.

3. Which TWO good images and ONE bad image does Paul use to describe the Christian life in verses 7-9 and 15?

4. How do you understand the phrase 'the offence of the Cross'?

Chapter 14

LIFE IN THE SPIRIT
Galatians Chapter 5 verses 16-26.

In this letter, Paul is responding to the false teachers who have infiltrated the Galatian churches, rubbishing his credential as an apostle, and saying that his gospel is inadequate, and required the additions of legalist performance in the matter of Jewish ceremony. This is of course relevant to us today because it raises the whole question of whether we have spiritual peace through what we can do for God, or through accepting and believing in what God has done for us in His grace through the sacrifice of the Lord Jesus Christ on the Cross for our sins. Paul is very concerned that the Galatians, who were born free in Christ, are having their free birthright undermined in a way which will redirect them back to their pagan slavery to sin and inadequacy.

The apostle Paul is very concerned about the Galatian Christians, and uses his mighty, dedicated intellect to attack the position of his opponents. In the first two chapters of the letter he does it personally, and in the second two chapters he does it theologically. We are in the third section where he does it practically, recalling them to God's wonderful freedom, like the skilled conductor of an orchestra bringing them back to the main theme of the symphony. Chapter 5 verse 1 says; 'For freedom Christ has set us free. Stand firm, then and do not let yourselves be burdened again by a yoke of slavery.' Chapter five continues by demonstrating how they have been interrupted and side-tracked, and how practical Christian freedom is in directing us to self-control, loving service to our neighbour, any person in need thrown across our path, and, in an obedience to the law of God inspired and enabled by the indwelling Holy Spirit of God.

The Christian life is described as 'walk' in verse 16, where the verb is translated 'live' in the New International Version. 'Walk' is a good word, implying a dynamic, controlled, steady progress. Paul uses this word in Romans 6 verse 4 to describe our new life in Christ, a life directed by the power of the Holy Spirit (Romans 8 verse 6.) This personal regulation of the pace of life is contrary to the urges and drives of the sinful nature mentioned in verse 17. 'Sinful nature' is literally 'flesh', normally used of a life governed by appetite, or self-satisfaction, including here a proud attitude concerning our personal achievement in law-keeping performance. There is an implacable conflict between the gratification of the flesh on the one hand, and the life of grace energised by the Spirit, on the other hand.

We'll have to dig a little deeper into the ugly display of the sinful nature and the beautifully balanced harvest of the Spirit

In this section, if they did not know it before, **Christians are described as clearly on a war footing.** Paul writes in verses 17 and 18: 'For the sinful nature desires what is contrary to the Spirit, and the Spirit what is contrary to the sinful nature. They are in conflict with each other, so that you do not do what you want.' There are some Christians who would claim to have no sense of this inner conflict, who have had some inner experience of the Holy Spirit which has removed them from all this. They feel, as the old hymn says, 'shut in with Thee , far far above the restless world which wars below', and oblivious to the conflict other Christians experience. They would say that the warfare described in Romans chapter 7 is foreign to their experience. In Romans chapter 7 verses 21-25, Paul writes: 'So I find this law at work; when I want to do good, evil is right there with me. For in my inner being I delight in God's law; but I see another law at work in the members of my body, waging war against the law of my mind and making me a prisoner of the law of sin at work within my members. What a wretched man I am! Who will rescue me from this body of death? Thanks be to God – through Jesus Christ our Lord! So then I myself in my mind am a slave to God's law, but in the sinful nature a slave to the law of sin.' I find experience echoes this conflict situation. There is deliverance, and God has provided spiritual armour for the conflict with Satan and the spiritual powers of darkness, as

Ephesians chapter 6 verses 10-18. I agree with Dr Alexander Whyte's verdict on the Christian life; 'It's a sair fecht (painful fight) until we get to the pearly gates.' There is a story about a native American, or Red Indian as they used to be known, who became a Christian and was asked what the Christian life was all about. He said it was like having two dogs, an evil dog , and a good dog, fighting inside him. And when he was asked which one was winning, he said 'the one I feed the most!'

In verses 19 to 21, Paul launches into an inventory of the overt acts of the sinful nature – sexual immorality, impurity and debauchery (sexual sins); idolatry and witchcraft (religious sins); hatred, discord, jealousy, fits of rage, selfish ambition, dissensions, factions and envy (social sins); drunkenness, orgies and the like (drinking sins).' This is the package which makes up a doomed and ugly life-style and it is not the total picture, as the phrase 'and the like indicates.'

The ancient world used to compile lists of good and bad acts, like the seven deadly sins, and the four cardinal virtues. Paul sometimes uses lists, like the virtues set out in Philippians 4 verses 8 and 9, or the qualities of love in 1 Corinthians 13 verses 4-7. Here, in vivid contrast to the previous verses, Paul lists the individual fruits which are components of the beautifully balanced harvest of the Spirit which results from our movement from being born free to living the life which embodies the freedom of God's grace.

Again, there is a composite package here, so it is good sense to use the collective noun 'fruit of the Spirit', rather than 'fruits of the Spirit'. It is interesting too note the contrast between Paul's description of the facets of the sinful nature as 'acts', or 'works' and the facets of life in the (Holy) Spirit as 'fruit'. It is the contrast between human activity and divine empowering. WE Vine says 'fruit is the visible expression of power working inwardly and invisibly, the character of the fruit being evidence of the character of the power producing it. As the visible expressions of hidden lusts are the works of the flesh, so the invisible power of those who are brought into living union with Christ produces 'the fruit of the Spirit', the singular form suggesting the unity of the character of the Lord reproduced in them.'

Verses 22 and 23 list the component fruits which make up the 'fruit of the Spirit'. Fruit is the natural overflow of a healthy tree or plant. It is futile and artificial to try tying the fruit on to the tree! I once heard about a keen golfer who discovered his golf balls were going missing, and he discovered his small boy had been watching dad planting potatoes, and was trying to produce a fruitful harvest of golf balls by planting some in the garden! Another thing to note is the emphasis here on character rather achievement or performance. The present-day stress seems to be on the fruit of the Spirit rather than the gifts of the Spirit. The gifts seem more attractive because some of them are spectacular, in contrast to the quiet growth of a godly character. Perhaps it is good to restore the balance by looking at this section in some detail.

Paul lists nine pieces of fruit in these verses, which John Stott of the orderly mind sorts into three triads of virtues – love joy and peace describing the fruit in relation to God, patience, kindness and goodness in relation to others, and faithfulness, gentleness and self-control in relation to ourselves.

Love stands at the head of the list, for elsewhere Paul says it summarises the demands of God's law (Galatians 5 verse 14), it outlasts even faith and hope in its enduring quality (1 Corinthians 13 verse 13), unites all the virtues of living (Colossians 3 verse 14), and flows out from God's Holy Spirit. 'Love' is an overworked word in the English language, used in a wide variety of contexts – I love strawberries, I love the moonlight, I love you. (Sometimes when people say 'I love you', they mean 'I love me, I want you'). The Greek language is more sensible. It has four basic words for love. Storgia is the word for affection, like you have for a pal or a pet. Philia is the warm family love we feel for our nearest and dearest. Eros is the physical passion of a man for a woman. It is never used in the New Testament. The fourth word is agape. William Barclay defines Agape love as 'unconquerable kindness', the word used here in Galatians. Agape wishes the highest good for the beloved, and includes the reason, or mind, as well as the emotions. Agape love is operational prior to any response on the part of the beloved. Paul writes in Romans 5 verse 7-8 'Very rarely will anyone die for righteous man, though for a good man someone might possibly dare to die. But God demonstrates His own love for us in this: while we were still sinners, Christ died for us'.

Agape was used exclusively of the Greek gods before the time of Jesus, but was minted as a new coin to be used by Christians as descriptive of their characteristic love.

The second fruit is **Joy.** It is a quality grounded in God rather than in human feelings. Joy was a trade-mark of the Early Church. The lifestyle of the early Christians immediately after Pentecost illustrates this: 'Every day they continued to meet together in the temple courts. They broke bread in their homes and ate together with glad and sincere hearts, praising God and enjoying the favour of all the people.' AT Robertson describes the joyful life emphasised in Paul's letter to the Philippians, which has 13 references to joy in four chapters, as 'a spiritual rhapsody'. Joy has to be distinguished from happiness, which can fluctuate according to circumstances or temperament. Joy is like the steady depths of the sea under the tossing waves on its surface. The great hymn-writer, an ex-slave-trader and seaman John Newton wrote a hymn which said 'with Christ in the vessel I can smile at the storm.'

The third fruit is **Peace,** used frequently by Jewish people in the conventional greeting 'shalom'. For the Christian who is living life energised by the Holy Spirit of God, the peace spoken of here is a positive gift rather than a conventional greeting. Paul uses a striking phrase 'peace through the blood of His Cross.' This peace is not mere absence of strife or struggle. It is the reality of a mind at ease coupled to a heart which is tranquil.

Now we have had a brief look at the first triad, seeing the fruit in relation to God.

The second triad contains three juicy fruits – patience, kindness and self-control.

Patience is a persistent and overcoming quality. The Greek word is used with regard to people rather than patience in relation to events and things. It is used of God's patient dealings with people, for example in Romans 9 verse 22: 'What if God, choosing to show His wrath and make His power known, bore

with great patience the objects of His wrath...'
Kindness and **Goodness** are fruits that grow together. **Kindness** has a mellow quality like matured wine. Jesus says in Matthew 11 verse 30 that His yoke is kind or easy, meaning the carpenter has lovingly smoothed out any knots or rough pieces in the wood so that the beast that wears it will find that it does not chafe or annoy. Kindness is utterly helpful.

Goodness is a comprehensive combination of kindness and strength. The three fruits mentioned here are powerful allies in building relationships with other people.

The third triad – faithfulness, gentleness and self-control are fruits which operate within a spiritual character, and provide powerful evidence of the Spirit of Jesus in a person.

Faithfulness has to do with reliability. The person who possesses it keeps his promises.

William Barclay says that the word translated **'Gentleness'** is the most untranslatable of words. It describes a person who demonstrates submission to the will of God combined with a teachable spirit. It is a characteristic balanced between extremes of anger and passivity. It is used of a beast that has been tamed, like a horse controlled by bit and bridle, with its strength held under discipline. Therefore this gentleness or meekness is not weakness, but controlled strength, epitomised in the Old Testament hero Moses, who could kill an Egyptian with his bare hands and bury him in the sand, but later on as a leader under God's control could be described as 'more humble than any man on the face of the earth'. (Numbers 12 verse 3). In the New Testament, Paul pleads with the Corinthian Christians 'by the meekness and gentleness of Christ (2 Corinthians 10 verse 1). .

Self-control or self-mastery is that quality exhibited by someone who has each thought and each temper held in check because of inner strength granted by the Holy Spirit.

Paul has set out the ugly multiplicity of the acts of the sinful nature and the beautiful harmony of the fruit which shows life in the Spirit. In verses 23 to 26, he says that a life like that fulfils the law apart from law (verse 23), provides convincing evidence that the sinful nature of a spiritual Christian has been crucified (verse 24), gives constant motivation for a daily walk with God (verse 25), and gives a good antidote for conceit, provocative and envious behaviour (verse 26). Ann Jervis says conceit is detrimental to participation in the Spirit, provocation is contrary to unity in the Spirit, and envy can be at the root of disruptive, aggressive and destructive behaviour. These traits may be particular problems for people who are contending for recognition of their spiritual gifts and who are striving for the upper hand in spirituality.

In the next chapter, we'll examine from chapter six the varied aspects of well-doing in the Christian life....

QUESTIONS FOR DISCUSSION 5 v 16-26

1. Contrast the two lifestyles described in chapter 5 v 16-18.

2. Attempt to group 'the acts of the sinful life' (5 v 16-18)

3. Attempt to group 'the fruit of the Spirit'. Is there any significant difference between 'fruit' and 'fruits'?

4. Can you describe positive and negative ways to 'live in the Spirit' from verses 25 and 26 ?

OUTLINE OF GALATIANS CHAPTER 6.

Paul gives a series of examples of Christian good deeds – restoring someone who has fallen into sin, sharing others' burdens, honest self-assessment and appropriate responsibility, sharing Christ's teaching, and recognising the sowing and reaping principle at the heart of all living. Paul urges persistence in good deeds, particularly towards fellow-Christians.

Paul personalises his writings here, and warns against the pro-circumcision pressure-group, who glory only in the flesh. Paul glories only in Christ's Cross, and underlines the governing authority of the 'one creation' principle in church life. He pleads to be left in peace as someone who bears the marks of Christ, and in the final section includes the blessings of peace, mercy and grace.

CHAPTER 15.

LIVING CREATIVELY
Galatians Chapter 6 verses 1-10

In this chapter, we are considering Galatians chapter 6, verses 1-10, and our heading is 'Living Creatively.' Let's hear it in the Eugene Peterson 'Message' translation, which is really a paraphrase:

'Live creatively, friends. If someone falls into sin, forgivingly restore him, saving your critical comments for yourself. YOU might be needing forgiveness before the day's out. Stoop down and reach out to those who are oppressed. . Share their burdens, and so complete Christ's law. If you think you are too good for that, you are badly deceived.

Make a careful exploration of who you are and the work you have been given, and then sink yourself into that. Don't be impressed with yourself. Don't compare yourself with others. Each of you must take responsibility for doing the creative best you can do with your own life.

Be very sure now, you who have been trained to a self-sufficient maturity, that you enter into a generous common life with those who have trained you, sharing all the good things that you have, and experience.

Don't be misled: no one makes a fool of God. What a person plants, he will harvest. The person who plants selfishness, ignoring the needs of others-ignoring God!- harvests a crop of weeds. All he'll have to show for his life is weeds! But the one who plants in response to God, letting God's Spirit do the growth work in him, harvests a crop of real life, eternal life.

So let's not allow ourselves to get fatigued doing good. At the right time we will harvest a good crop if we don't give up, or quit. Right now, therefore, every time we get the chance, let us work for the benefit of all, starting with the people closest to us in the community of faith.'

We are obviously looking at the practical section of Paul's letter.

In chapters one and two he had argued his case for a gospel of free and sovereign grace **personally**, and then in chapter three and four he had argued **theologically**. This section, in chapters 5 and 6, gives **practical** teaching about how to live creatively by the indwelling Spirit of God, and is chiefly about Christian well-doing. Martin Luther said: 'Good works do not make a good man, but a good man does good works.' To put good works before faith and grace, is like putting the cart before the horse.

Christians are sometimes described as 'do-gooders'. Unfortunately it is the 'do-badders' who make the headlines, and the headlines they make are not very encouraging, to say the least. It is probably right to comment on the good work done by Christians in Britain at a time when they are being ridiculed and marginalised, and Christian influence on our history and culture us being quietly air-brushed out by modern gurus. The Factory Acts, the Parliamentary Acts for the protection of chimney boys and children labouring in the mines, the slave abolitionist movement led by Wilberforce, the Secret Ballot Act of 1872 driven by William Ewart Gladstone, the Poverty Acts, pioneer work in scientific advance, medical care and education, Penal Reform, and Public Health, were largely carried through by Christians.

At this present time, there are large numbers of Christians supporting and complementing the work done by Social Work departments. Some churches have built care homes and nursing homes in their communities, established youth clubs, coffee mornings and lunch clubs, and organised respite centres for Alzheimer sufferers so that relatives can have a break. If we were to put end-to-end all the Go-Pak tables in use in Christian churches for the benefit of those needing support, they would encircle the planet! Yet people speak and write about Christians as if they were all obscurantist freaks. We need a chapter like Galatians 6 to show how those born free through the Gospel can express the love they have for God creatively and practically.

1. Living by the Spirit's power, we can do good to others. We could take **chapter 6 verse 9 as a headline text:** 'Let us not become weary in doing good, for at the proper time we will reap a harvest if we do not give up', and then look at the preceding

verses through this filter. The situations highlighted are the happy aftermath of the crucifixion of the sinful nature. They show that life in the Spirit works in live situations in which we aware of one another.

First of all, Paul illustrates creative living in the Spirit in **RESTORING THE FALLEN (verse 1).** ' Brothers, if someone is caught in a sin, you who are spiritual should restore him gently. But watch yourself, or you also may be tempted.' There is a contrast here between how a legalist would react to this situation and how a spiritual person would react. Warren Wiersbe says the legalist doesn't need proof or evidence – suspicion and rumours will do. The conditions are clearly explained by the apostle. Firstly, the 'caught' element indicates surprise, when the fallen person's guard was down. Secondly, the word used for sin is 'paraptoma', translated 'fault' in the King James Version. The Greek Old Testament usage means it is an oversight, or error. The Classical Greek usage means a blunder, or an unintentional mistake. The New Testament usage intensifies the meaning to indicate a deliberate act leading to judgement. In any case, the target is restoration. (it would be condemnation for a legalist). The Greek word for 'restore' (katartizo) means 'to put in order, to repair, to overhaul', and is used of fishermen repairing nets, so that the mesh is completely back in working order, in Matthew 4 verse 21, and is used in Classical Greek of a doctor resetting a dislocated limb. Both of these uses indicate a specialist task, so it is here only 'you who are spiritual' who are singled out for this job. John Stott says: 'one of the reasons why only spiritual Christians should attempt the ministry is that only the spiritual are gentle.' The other point is that, as the end of verse 1 makes clear success in this task can lead to the temptation to boast about it. Paul is as concerned about the restorer as the sinner.

This issue raises the question as to **the extent of restoration.** I have heard it argued that the pastoral ministry is an area where people who have fallen into serious moral sin should not glibly expect quick restoration so that full service is resumed as soon as possible. I have also heard Christians argue that pastors involved in sexual sin have disqualified themselves from ever again being pastors. Their basis has been 1 Corinthians 9 verse

26: 'Therefore I do not run like a man running aimlessly; I do not fight like a man beating the air. No, I beat my body and make it my slave so that after I have preached to others, I myself will not be disqualified from the prize.' These Christians have said that the position of trust a pastor is in, and the lack of supervision of his activities mean that he can not resume these duties. Some Christian groups will not allow divorced persons to engage in front-line ministry. Other Christians say that the term 'restore' here means just that, and a divorced person can become a pastor, or missionary, or even a presenter on Christian radio, provided they truly repent and are restored to living and walking in step with the Spirit

We move on to **BEARING THE BURDENS** in verse 2, where Paul writes: 'Carry each other's burdens and in this way you will fulfil the law of Christ.' The key word here is the word 'Burdens' (ta baree). This word means a heavy load, and there is no contradiction between carrying another's burden in verse 2 and carrying our own load in verse 5. The word translated 'load' in verse 5 is 'phortion' which is used of a soldier's pack. Many Christians find from time to time that they have to carry an oppressive load – a sick relative, an unconverted and unsympathetic husband or wife, a rebellious child, a personal illness – and it is good for a sensitive and spiritual fellow-Christian to get alongside them and provide a helpful shoulder! Martin Luther says in his commentary on this verse: 'Christians need broad shoulders and mighty bones to bear the burden.' The 'soldier's pack' imagery of verse 5 means a load appropriate to our strength and spiritual maturity.

Verses 3-5 refer to TAKING THE RESPONSIBILITIES. Verse 3 calls for straight self-assessment, without the constant fruitless activity of comparing ourselves with others. Paul says in Romans 12 verse 3 : 'think your way to a sober estimate of yourself,based on faith.' (New English Bible). There are personal responsibilities which relate to ourselves. Warren Wiersbe says : 'If my car breaks down, my neighbour can help drive my children to school, but he cannot assume the responsibilities that only belong to me as a father.'

In chapter 6 verse 6, Paul writes about SHARING THE BLESSING. Teachers of the Word have a special responsibility to share what they have been given, so that the blessing flows on across the generations. The message given from the podium or pulpit must be a two-way experience, with mutual sharing of the good things of God, and the teaching that is given must be earthed in the experience of God's people. That is why pulpiteers or evangelists who live remote and unnatural lives sometimes go 'off the rails' in their evangelical orthodoxy, or even their moral behaviour. In their pulpits, they are 'six feet above contradiction' – or correction. They have cut themselves off from the healthy correctives which come from their fellow Christians,. Rev George Duncan told me he had refused several offers from America to go and become a 'pulpiteer', for this very reason.

Similarly, those who receive Christian instruction should not make their favourite preachers, teachers into icons or idols. They should recognise their responsibilities, like the Bereans in Acts 17 verse 10, 'for they received the message with great eagerness, and examined the Scriptures every day to see if what Paul said was true.' Galatians 6 verse 6 was especially useful for the Galatian believers under the threat of false teachers.

We are looking at the practical section of the Letter to the Galatians, and at chapter 6 verses 1-10, where Paul is discussing living creatively in the Spirit. So far, we have looked at Restoring the Fallen (verse 1), Bearing the Burden (verse 2), Taking the Responsibility (verses 3-5), and Sharing the Blessing (verse 6). In the summing-up section, **verses 7-10, he is looking at REAPING THE HARVEST.** Let's recall the section in the Message translation: 'Don't be misled. No one makes a fool of God. What a person plants, he will harvest. The person who plants selfishness, ignoring the needs of others – ignoring God- harvests a crop of weeds! All he'll have to show for his life is weeds! But the one who plants in response to God, letting God''s Spirit do the growth work in him, harvests a crop of real, eternal life.'

The sowing and reaping principle operates in various areas of life. A crisp-guzzling couch potato will jeopardise his health and fitness, and bring increased pressure to his medical advisers and sadness, and perhaps financial distress, to his family. Lazy students have been known to fail exams. Parents who have failed to discipline their children may reap heartache as they are called up to meet school authorities about their naughty children. Someone said: 'Don't say 'O those naughty children!' Say 'O those incompetent parents!'

The solemnity of the issues of life are set out here. The Bible says: 'Don't be misled. No one makes a fool of God'.

Imagine if there were some people listening to this who think that they can mock God by the lives they live, deliberately. Or imagine this: there could be people listening to this who are unwittingly mocking God by the way they live. There may be time to repent of this and change direction, but the warning is clear here. The late Revd George B Duncan preached on this passage under the following headlines: (headings his, comments mine).

1. Living is Sowing. Our actions seem isolated but results will be implicated.

I think he meant that we are affected by the moral and philosophical climate we live in. People say it is unfair and unrealistic to expect consistency in our behaviour. Our feelings fluctuate, and so do our moods and tempers. How I act today need have no connection with how I acted last week, nor any bearing on how I will act next week. However much we try to dodge responsibility it is true that we sow a thought and reap an action, we sow an action and reap a character, and we sow a character and reap a destiny.

2. Living is Choosing. There is a restricted choice, and there is a responsible choice.

To illustrate in Bible terms what the good George B Duncan meant, we live in an ethos of strong contrasts: good and evil, light and darkness, the wide gate and the restricted gate, the broad way and the narrow way, the kingdom of darkness and the kingdom of God's dear Son, the sinful nature and the Spirit's guidance. Therefore choose life, that our souls may live. The

Bible teaches that there is a heaven to gain and a hell to shun.

3. Living is Growing. The nature of living leads to development, and the numbers in living warns us of involvement.

Our characters grow and develop according to our behaviour. In that awful but gripping book by Oscar Wilde 'The Picture of Dorian Gray', published in 1890, Dorian makes a deal that his handsome and dashing image will not change, but the effects of his dissolute behaviour will instead appear in his portrait hidden in an attic. The shock of seeing his depraved portrait was too much for him. Dr Alexander Maclaren of Manchester was a fine preacher whose Sunday morning sermon was published in full in the Monday morning issue of the 'Manchester Guardian'. In one of his sermons, he graphically describes someone in hell, surrounded like an actor on stage by his audience, which consisted of the fully-grown evil thoughts he had produced. Things develop in our lives and whether the development is good or bad, others are implicated in what David the psalmist called 'the bundle of life.'

4. Living is Reaping. The contrast we see here brings us face to face with the caution we face here.

Our actions in life determine our outcomes in life, and everything is naked and open in the eyes of God. Once we have finished sowing, we cannot change the harvest. In the world of Christian service, if every believer regarded his material wealth as seed , and planted it prayerfully and thoughtfully, there would be no lack of money to engage in Christ's service. The seed must also include the content and teaching of the Word of God.

If we sow to please and pander to our sinful nature, we will reap destruction. If, however, we sow to please the Spirit, and do God's will, we will reap eternal life. Paul rounds off the section by promising a harvest in verse 9, 'at the proper time.? We should neither attempt to fool God nor ourselves, and get on with the work of sowing.

In verse 10, Paul singles out the household of faith for special treatment. These are our fellow-believers home and abroad, who through trusting in God's grace are also part of His family, for whom charity begins at home.

QUESTIONS FOR DISCUSSION 6 v 1-10

1. Give THREE qualities requires when helping a fallen brother or sister? (6 v 1)

2. What is 'the law of Christ'? And how can we fulfil it?

3. Is there a contradiction between verse 2 and verse 5?

4. Does the sowing and reaping principle relate only To our human life-span?

CHAPTER 16.

THE CROSS OF CHRIST AND THE MARKS OF CHRIST. GALATIANS CHAPTER 6 VERSES 11-18.

In this chapter we look at the final section of the letter, chapter 6 verses 11-18, under the heading 'The Cross of Christ and the Marks of Christ.' You will spot immediately that the talk spins around two centres, verse 14 and verse 17, and that we will give only minor treatment to the rest of the passage. We are still in the third part of the letter, having had the PERSONAL PART in chapters 1 and 2, and the DOCTRINAL PART in chapters 3 to 4, and finish off dealing with the PRACTICAL PART in chapters 5 and 6. The last two chapters are helpful in pointing out some of the results of grace in the Christian lives of the Galatians. They have been saved by grace alone by faith in Christ alone, and have been Born Free as the children of the free woman Sarah (chapter 4 verse 31). Their new birth by the power of the Holy Spirit (chapter 4 verse 29) has brought them a new liberty from law-keeping and ritual performance in an attempt to please God through law-keeping. This new identity now has to be expressed in a new behaviour as they keep in step with the Spirit (chapter 5 verse 24).

The Greek world had set forms for ending letters as well as beginning them. Some writers used an amanuensis, or secretary. The writer would round things off by summarising its content in his own handwriting. Again, we can use a musical analogy, for this pattern is like a composer recapitulating the main themes of a symphony as it comes to an end. The cowardly ways of the false teachers appear in verses 12 and 13. The centrality of the Cross and the new creation seen in their new birth are mentioned in verses 14 and 15 , are followed by a first benediction on the new people of God (verse 16) and a reference to Christ's marks in verse 17, and a second benediction on God's family, verse 18.

The statement in verse 14 translated 'May I never boast, except in the cross of the Lord Jesus Christ' is a powerful denial. The Greek expression 'me genoito' can be translated 'perish the thought that' or 'away with the whole idea that', 'let it never come to pass that'. This raises one of the key questions of the whole Bible: What are we glorying in? This is a good test for us throughout our Christian lives. Pride can show itself in several ways:

1. PRIDE OF FACE (The Lookers). Those who have good looks, and good physical appearance sometimes boast in this. We have a burgeoning beauty industry in our country generating millions of pounds in revenue each year. Nowadays, politicians are selected partly because of their suitability for television, so that they LOOK good.

2. PRIDE OF RACE (The Bigots). These people are rabid nationalists, and often talk down other races by inventing nicknames for them, like Krauts or Huns , Nips, Spades, Spics and Wogs. Of course when we point the finger at others there are three pointing at ourselves.

3. PRIDE OF PLACE (The Climbers). These are the people who are involved in the cut-throat rat-race for status. Programmes like 'The Apprentice' on television, and films like 'The Firm' make people aware of luxury cars, fine clothes, high-quality houses, six-figure salaries and job promotion.

4. PRIDE OF GRACE (The Pharisees and their modern equivalents). Spiritual pride is probably the worst kind of pride, epitomised in Robert Burns' poem entitled 'Holy Willie's Prayer', and in Scripture in the Lord Jesus' parable about 'the Pharisee and the Tax-collector'. The context here in Galatians is about the false teachers who gloried in circumcision. Paul wants to glory only in the Cross, as we have seen. He meditates on the Cross, and this makes him face up to things in three different ways:

1. HE FACES UP TO THE CROSS.

2. HE FACES UP TO THE WORLD.

3. HE FACES UP TO HIMSELF.

Let us face up to each of these three in detail.

Paul is taken up in this letter with the Person of the Cross. The Lord Jesus Christ is referred to about forty times in the space of about 150 verses, and the Cross is mentioned specifically about six times. Paul faces up to the Cross as an antidote to pride in several ways. He probably thought of it like most other folk, as a hated symbol of Roman domination, a cruel instrument of torture and death, the mode of death penalty which the Romans borrowed from the Persians. The apostle Peter refers to it as 'the lump of wood' (xulon, 1Peter 2 v 24) rather than the cross (stauros). Death on a Cross was painful and public, demeaning and humiliating. The victim's resistance was softened up by scourging, the cross was not usually a fine piece of varnished wood, but a section hacked from a tree trunk. The victim was tied or, in our Lord's case, nailed to the cross, with ugly, square-sectioned nails driven through the butt of the hands, and slamming the cross into the ground would dislocate both shoulders. Crucifixions took place in public, the victim was further humiliated by being stripped, and eventually the heat, the hunger and thirst, and asphyxiation through physical weakness led to the welcome relief of death. The Acts preaching of the Cross is restrained, and does not dwell on the sufferings of Christ pictured in the 'Stations of the Cross', but Peter, for instance says; 'You killed the Author of Life, but God raised Him from the dead.' (Acts 3 verse 15).

As Paul gloried in the Cross, he would doubtless think about the cost of His sins, the price of His pardon in the shed blood of the Saviour, the breadth of God's indiscriminate love, and the quality of God's Son. These thoughts should inspire us too as we meditate on what it cost God to redeem sinners like us, and this should lead us to say 'thanks' and to glory in a great and gracious God. Paul Gerhardt, the Lutheran mystic, and one of the greatest hymn-writers of German Protestantism, wrote the following hymn:

'Extended on a cursed tree, besmeared with dust, and sweat, and blood,
See there, the King of Glory, see! Sinks and expires the Son of God.
Who, who, my Saviour, this hath done? Who could thy sacred body wound?
No guilt Thy spotless heart hath known, no guile hath in Thy lips been found.
I, I alone, have done the deed! 'tis I Thy sacred flesh hath torn;
My sins have caused Thee, Lord, to bleed, Pointed the nail, and fixed the thorn.
The burden, for me to sustain too great, on Thee, my Lord, was laid;
To heal me, thou hast borne my pain; to bless me, Thou a curse was made.
My Saviour, how shall I proclaim? How pay the mighty debt I owe?
Let all I have and all I am, ceaseless to all Thy glory show.
Too much to thee I cannot give; too much I cannot do for Thee;
Let all Thy love, and all Thy grief, graven on my heart for ever be!'

Paul not only faced up to the Cross, but **he faced up to the world.** There are two general uses of the word 'world' in the New Testament. The first one refers to the world created by God, the ordered kosmos, where we can see all things bright and beautiful on the one hand, or 'nature red in tooth and claw' on the other. One of the philosophers called our life on planet earth 'a dysteleological surd' i.e. 'an aimless, unbalanced existence'.

The second use of the word is as a description of a world hostile to God, the organised, sinful, anti-God system around us, which is full of implacable hate against the Lord, and against His Christ. Most commentators agree that it is this second meaning which is presented here. Paul as a preacher had been at the receiving end of insults, rejection, beatings, stoning, and imprisonment because he was a servant of Christ and His Gospel. All Christians are people in tension – in the world, but not of it. Christians are, to use John Stott's phrase, part of a subversive counter-culture, and are like salmon swimming against the stream, onward and upward. Paul was aware of the world's standards and the world's attractions and the world's dangers, and as far as he was concerned, the world was crucified to him. He and we had and have three responsibilities to the world. Firstly, we should **pity the world,** as Jesus did when He saw people who were like sheep without a shepherd. As His heart compassion moved him to action, so we should love our God-hating neighbours and enemies, and move out to help everyone in need thrown across our path. Secondly, we should **pray for the world.** Every one killed or maimed by a land-mine that goes off in Afghanistan, and every teenager stabbed in the cities of Britain, should drive us to God to pray for the sad world in which we live. Thirdly, we should **penetrate the world,** and find a way to reach out to the world and influence the people of this world in which we live. I pray that God will reach out to some of you, so that you can experience the love of Jesus as you read this.

Paul says that the world has been crucified to him, and he to the world. Some folk think this is just an example of tautology, that is, saying the same thing over again in different words. I don't think this is the case. The first phrase 'by whom, or by which the world has been crucified to me' focuses on Paul's view and valuation of the world, and the second phrase 'and I to the world' focuses on Paul's view and valuation of himself. The Cross, and the Christ of the Cross, had changed Paul. He had what some Christians call the two degrees – BA, and MA – that is Born Again, and Marvellously Altered. What had happened to him is what happens to any Christian. The experience of the real thing, the sense of liberty peace and forgiveness, the sense of being born free, meant that he would never be the same again. Jesus had spoiled him for the world. He could never go back, and find joy in what he was before. This sense of forgiveness was meant to be a permanent thing. There was only one safe place to be- under the shadow of Christ's cross, in the centre of His will, and in the fellowship of His church. There is no substitute for salvation!

This leads him in this final summary section to what some have called the New Creation principle, following verse 15 : 'neither circumcision nor uncircumcision means anything; what counts is a new creation.' Belief in a new creation in the lives of sinful human beings brings peace, mercy, and a sense of unity with God's people past and present, so that he calls the church the Israel of God, meaning that believers in the Lord Jesus Christ are the true inheritors of God's purposes, and part of God's 'salvation-history.' There was an ongoing battle in the first century between two rival camps, one that argued for surrender to Christ, and one that argued for surrender to Christ AND Moses. Paul's argument in Galatians is that the law of Moses reached its climax in Christ, whose holy life and painful sacrifice pointed the way ahead so that people believing in Christ would live a life inspired by the Spirit, a life which was a new creation, where faith would be energised into holiness and service.

In l verse, 17, Paul in a final thrust at the false teachers points to the authentic evidence of a true Christian. This is not the surgical scar of circumcision, but the marks of Jesus expressed in sacrificial living resulting from identifying with the Lord Jesus. Paul says he bears in his body 'the marks of Jesus'. Down the centuries, people have claimed for themselves, or others have claimed for saintly people they have admired, that the scars inflicted on the Lord Jesus have reappeared in physical manifestations in their flesh. Sometimes, these **stigmata** appear on one area or a few areas of a person's skin, like the palms of the hands, or the forehead to replicate the marks made by the crown of thorns, or the shoulders because of Christ's bearing of the Cross, or on their back, where Jesus was scourged. There have been over three hundred such claims, including such people as Francis of Assisi. Some have dismissed these as the result of auto-suggestion. Others have described, in eye-witness accounts, the dark encrusted areas of the skin, which have exuded blood, so that others have spoken of neuropathic bleeding. Some have claimed that Paul is first in the line of those who had these manifestations. They point to evidence of his mystic experiences in 2 Corinthians chapter 12, and claim

Paul had replica prints of the nails which pierced the Lord in his own hands. William Barclay points out the thrust of what Paul says here was culturally relevant. He says: 'Often a master branded his slaves with a mark that showed them to be his.

'Most likely what Paul means is that the scars and marks of the things he had suffered for Christ are the brands which show him to be the slave of Christ. In the end it is not his apostolic authority he uses as a basis of appeal; it is the wounds he bore for Christ's sake. Like Mr Valiant-for-Truth in 'Pilgrim's Progress', Paul could say: 'My marks and scars I carry with me to be my witness to Him who will now be my rewarder.' He catalogues them in 2 Corinthians 11 verses 23 to 25, including stoning, being left for dead in the gutter, five times being given thirty-nine lashes, and three occasions when he was beaten with rods.

I remember meeting and talking with Richard Wurmbrandt at the Keswick Convention on a beautiful day in July. He told the small group I was with that he had a number of scars (I think it was thirteen) on his body. These were inflicted by his torturers during his years of imprisonment in Rumanian jails because of his Christian faith and work as a pastor. It was almost surreal to think of such things in the beauty of an English summer in the Lake District. We should remember that living as a Christian is not 'a cream tea', but can be a 'baptism of fire.' 'Show me your scars'....

Paul finishes the letter with that sunshine word 'grace.' 'The grace of our Lord Jesus be with your spirit, brothers. Amen.' The whole message of the letter had been about God's grace. It was **authenticating** grace which had taken a brilliant but bigoted Pharisee into a faith relationship with the risen Christ. It had been **transforming grace** which had made him into a missionary apostle, tempered in the furnace of suffering to face any kind of adversary. It had been **compassionate grace** which brought him in racking pain to proclaim the Gospel to the Galatians, and see them share his experience of God's mercy. It was **equipping grace** which made him so able to marshal arguments to show the dangers of following the false teachers who were trying to drive the born free Galatians back to the hamster-cage bondage of law-keeping and ritual. It was **justifying grace** which lay at the heart of his Gospel, so that sinful pagans and proud Pharisees could be fit to face God as reconciled sinners, and live glorying in that Cross which had been placarded before their very eyes. It was Christ's **liberating grace** which set them free from the curse of the law by becoming a curse for them. It was **personal grace** which responded to their personal faith in Christ so that like Paul they too could say 'He loved me and gave Himself for me.' It was **familial grace** which brought them into step with Father Abraham who had also believed in life from the dead, and into step with people of every colour and class, knocking down all the conventional barriers which naturally separated them from each other.

What a letter! What a Gospel! What a Saviour! We have the same message of redeeming love and a new creation to give to the people of our generation. We have to tell them that they cannot, and needn't even try to work their passage to God, by adding giving to charity, or entering into special experiences to maintain acceptance with God. In a missionary context, nationals don't have to adopt Western models of church and churchmanship. They can come to God as they are, and respond to His grace, and worship and serve His Son by grace alone through faith alone, in ways appropriate to their culture.

QUESTIONS FOR DISCUSSION
6 v 11-18.

1.   What does it mean to 'boast in the Cross'?   (verse 14)

2.   Who do think 'the Israel of God' are?

3.   What 'marks of Jesus' did Paul carry? As Christians, should we expect to suffer? In what ways?
I hope that you have had some benefit from our teaching about Galatians, and pray that God will bless you and your homes and your families and your churches.

DIGGING DEEPER –
SOME TEXTUAL POINTS FROM THE
LETTER TO THE GALATIANS.

Before I launch into more technical matters, a word about language and grammar which may be helpful. The New Testament was originally written in Greek, which was widespread in the Mediterranean world. They used Common, or Koine Greek, which was a simplified form of Classical Greek, used by the common people.

• The PRESENT TENSE in Greek denotes present action, continuous or undefined. Eg 'I study' or 'I am studying'. Or John 6 v 35 'I am the Bread of life', continually.

• The FUTURE TENSE indicates action which has still to come (will/shall), either Predictive (Colossians 3 v 4) or Prescriptive eg 'a man will leave' Matthew 19 v 5.

• The PERFECT TENSE indicates past completed action which has continuing effects in the present, eg 'It is finished' John 13 verse 30 is in the perfect tense in Greek. Because Jesus fully completed His task, the ongoing effects are that we are offered the benefits of His finished work here and now.

• The IMPERFECT TENSE indicates past continuous, repeated or habitual action. eg 'I...persecuted the church of God' . It was Paul's regular habit to do so.

• The AORIST TENSE indicates undefined action, usually in the past. Some see it as a 'point' or 'punctiliar' tense, stating the fact of a decisive action without specifying its duration. Eg Colossians 3 v3 ' for you died' (Aorist), and your life has been hidden (and still is, Perfect) with Christ in God'.

• VOICE. English has two voices – active eg 'Bill hit the ball' and passive 'Bill was hit by the ball'. Greek has a third Voice, the Middle Voice, which is versatile in its use and meaning. It is mostly active, and is not necessarily reflexive. There is usually some effect on the subject. The active verb 'I ask' in the middle indicates 'I ask (for myself)'. If the active verb is 'I find', in the Middle Voice it means 'I obtain (for myself).'

• MOOD. This defines the relationship between the verb and reality. A verb is indicative if it is describing something that 'is' rather than something that 'may' or 'might' be.

• SUBJUNCTIVE MOOD. This mood is used when a verb expresses a possibility, probability, purpose, exhortation, a wish, a condition, or a certainty/uncertainty. Eg 'they shall never perish' (John 10 verse 28).
'I may learn Greek'. 'If I were a rich man, I would hire a Greek tutor.'
'so that the righteousness of the law might be fulfilled in us'.
'What should we eat?' 'What should we drink? What should we wear?' (Matthew 6 v 31).

• DEPONENT = a verb middle or passive in form, but active in meaning. In the present tense, middle and passive are identical in form, eg erchomai = 'I come'. 75% of middle forms in NT are Deponent in form.

In transliterating Greek words, I have represented 'eta' the long vowel 'e' by a double 'e', and omega, the long vowel 'o' by a double 'o'.
The pronunciation of 'eta' is like the vowel in 'fate' rather than the 'ee' in 'cheese', and the pronunciation of 'omega' is like the vowel in 'tone' rather than 'foot'.

NOTES ON CHAPTER ONE.

(United Bible Societies' Greek Text and New International Version)

1v1 'from men'..... 'by man' = 'ap' anthroopoon...di' anthroopou' =neither from a human origin, or through a human channel.
There is a subtle distinction in the use of the prepositions 'from' and 'through', and in the plural 'human beings' distinguished from 'a human beging'.
'who raised' = egeirantos = aorist participle, a decisive act, from 'egeiroo', frequently used in NT for waking up, or raising, from the sleep of death.

1v3 "grace'='charis'. In the OT it is the positive approval of the righteous before God (eg Genesis 6v8). In the NT grace is most often an unmerited, God-initiated kindness given from God's lvoing heart and hand, rather than as a return or reward.

1v4 'for our sins'= 'huper toon hamartioon'. Some manuscripts have 'peri' for 'huper'. Usually 'huper' is used for persons, and 'peri' for things.
'to rescue us' = 'hopoos exeleetai'. 'exeleetai' is a 2nd aorist subjunctive middle. The verb means 'to pluck out, rescue'. Lightfoot says 'this strikes the keynote of the epistle. The gospel is a rescue, an emancipation from the state of bondage.'
'evil'= 'poneerou'. The position of the word gives emphasis to it.

1v6 'so quickly'='houtos tacheoos'. The reference is to speed rather than time interval. The Galatians were apparently keen to change.
'deserting' = 'metatithesthe' = present middle indicative of 'metatitheemi' = to transfer = 'you are transferring yourselves'.
'heteron' 'a different gospel' = 'heteros' euanggelion'. See 2 Corinthians 11v4.
Another = distinct from, rather than 'allo'= another the same

as, which appears in verse 7, 'is no (gospel)' = 'ouk allo'.

1v7   'throwing you into confusion' = 'hoi tarassontes' = 'the disturbers' 'the stirrers' Used in Acts 17 v 8.
'to pervert'='metastrepsai'='to twist around'.

1v8   'if we' = 'ean heemeis' 'or an angel' = 'ee angelos'. He includes himself, and states not even an angel could change his position now.
'eternally condemned' = 'anathema'. = a thing devoted to God without being redeemed, doomed to destruction. He calls down a curse on anyone who proclaims a gospel to them contrary to the gospel they had heard from Paul.
In OT, Joshua 7 records how Achan's theft of anathema objects brought the whole nation into a state of anathema, and into defeat by Ai. It was a corporate responsibility issue. In the Early Church, the verb 'anathematizein' was modified later to mean 'excommunicate'.

1v10   'trying to win the approval' = 'peithoo', reckoned as a conative present tense, that is, it has the element of 'willing' or 'trying' to persuade.
'trying to please'= 'zeetoo . . . areskein' Here, effort is stated plainly. See 2 Corinthians 5v11.

1v11   'the gospel which was preached' = 'to euanggelion to euanggelisthen' = 'the gospel which was gospelized'   Play on words for emphasis.
The gospel Paul preached was 'kata theon', i.e. divine, or superhuman.

1v12   'Not from any man'= 'oude....para anthroopou' neither Peter, or any other apostle, nor School of Gamaliel, but 'by revelation' = 'di' apokalupseoos' directly from Jesus Christ.

1v13   'how intensely' = 'kath' huperboleen' = 'according to extremes, throwing beyond'
'I persecuted' = 'ediookon', and 'I tried to destroy it'. = 'eporthoun' are both imperfect tenses, indicating habitual activity.

'eporthoun' occurs again in 1v23.

1v14 'I was advancing' = 'proekopton' , another imperfect, 'I used to blaze a trail' . The verb prokoptoo = 'to cut forward' as in a forest. The leading scholar became the leading persecutor.

1v15 'who set me apart' = ' ho aphorisas' = aorist participle, from 'apo' = 'from'   plus 'horos' = 'a boundary line'   Romans 1v1.
'aphorizoo' is used in 2v12 to describe Peter's withdrawal from the Gentile meal-table.

1v16 'I did not confer' = 'ou prosanethemeen' , is a double compound = 'to take oneself to another', ie to seek a second opinion.

1v18. 'to get acquainted with' = 'historeesai , first aorist infinitive = to find out by visiting'. Only here in NT.
The Latin Vulgate has 'videre'='to see'. In Classical Greek, the word is related to 'historia'= 'an inquiry', the origin of the English word 'history'.

1v20 'is no lie' = 'ou pseudomai'. Serious enough matter for a solemn oath.

1v21 'ta klimata tees surias kai tees kalilias'='the area of Syria and Cilicia'. This was Paul's home territory. 'klimata' meant 'slopes' and became a technical description of the geographical strips defining the ancient world.

1v22. 'I was (personally) unknown' –'eemeen agnooumenos' - imperfect indicates continuous unawareness.
'personally'='too prosoopoo'='by face'.

NOTES ON CHAPTER TWO.

2v1 'later' = 'epeita dia'. 'dia' for time interval is normal usage.

2v2 ' in response to a revelation' = 'kata apokalupsin'. In Acts 15v2, the church sent them. There needn't be an inconsistency here.
'set before'='anethemeen'='I imparted' not 'I consulted' which would be 'prosanthemeen'. See 1v16.
'who seemed'='dokousin'=those who were reckoned as important.' There is no doubt or derogatory sense here.
'for fear that I was running in vain' = 'mee poos eis kenon trechoo ee edramon'. Negative purpose with present subjunctive of 'trechoo' then sudden change to aorist indicative 'edramon' = 'I had run', as a kind of afterthought.

2v3 'to be circumcised' = 'peritmeetheenai'. No grounds for arguing that Titus was circumcised voluntarily.

2v4 'false brothers'='pareisaktous'. Cleopatra's father, Ptolemy VI, was nicknamed 'Pareisaktos'='Substitute-on-the-Side', in relation to some dynastic skullduggery.
'to spy on' = 'kataskopeesai' first aorist passive infinitive of 'kataskopeoo' = 'to spy, reconnoitre, make a treacherous investigation.'
'to make us slaves' = katadouloosousin= future active indicative 'to enslave completely.' The case of Timothy was quite different – he had a Jewish mother and a Greek father. Titus was pure Greek.

2v6 'by external appearance'='prosoopon ... lambanei' 'does (not) receive the face', which in the NT always has the bad sense of partiality or favouritism.

2v8 'who was at work'= 'ho energeesas'. Hume says the surgeon who operates was known as 'ho energoon', and the patient being operated on was known as 'ho energoumenos'.

2v9 'pillars' = 'stulai', an old word for pillars or columns. (1

Timothy 3 v 15).
'right hand .... of fellowship' = 'dexias...koinoonias'
Compromisers and Judaisers were brushed to one side when
these five men shook hands as equals in the work of Christ's
kingdom.

2v10 'to continue to remember' = 'mneemoneuoomen' present
active subjunctive...'that we should keep on remembering'.

2v11 'he was...in the wrong' = 'kategnoosmenos een' periphrastic
(roundabout) perfect passive of 'kataginoskoo' = 'to know
against, find fault with'.

2v12 'he began to draw back' ='hupestellen'.....separate
(himself) = 'aphoorizen' both verbs are inchoative (initial,
undeveloped) imperfects.

2v13 'joined him in hypocrisy' = 'sunapeechthee' first aorist
passive indicative of 'sunapago', an old verb only here and 2
Peter 3v17. In Polybius = 'to act a part with'

2v14 'they were not acting in line' = 'ouk orthopodousin'
present indicative active retained in indirect discourse 'they
are not walking straight' or 'upright'.
'you force' = anangkazeis'. Conative (desire or attempt to
perform an action) present tense.

2v15 'Jews by birth' = 'phusei Ioudaioi'. Peter and Paul were
born and bred as Jews. They were not proselytes, or 'incomers'.
'Gentile sinners' = 'ethnoon hamartoloi' Jews regarded all
Gentiles as 'sinners' in comparison with themselves. (Matthew
26v45)

2v16 'a man is not justified' = 'ou dikaioutai anthroopos'
'dikaioutai'= present passive indicative of 'dikaioo' = 'to make,
declare righteous'. Formed like 'axiooo' = 'to deem worthy', and
'koinooo' = 'to consider common'. Two ways of attempting to
get right with God: 1. by faith in Christ Jesus 2. by keeping all
the law in the minutest fashion, the way of the Pharisees. Paul

knew them both, see his first recorded sermon in Acts 13v39. The four terms – faith, righteousness, law and works, occur more frequently in Galatians and Romans because of the issues Paul was dealing with there.

2v17 'it becomes evident' = ' heuretheemen'. 'we discover' ...when Jews or Gentiles come closer to Christ, their 'sinnership' becomes more obvious.
'absolutely not' = 'mee genoito' strong negative with the optative mood = mood of wishing 'may it not come to pass'.

2v18 'a lawbreaker' = 'parabateen' When he lived like a Gentile, he broke the ceremonial law. When he lived like a Jew, he tore down salvation by grace.

2v20 'I have been crucified' = 'sunestauroomai' perfect passive indicative of 'sustauroo' with the associative instrumental case ' Christoo' = 'with Christ.' One of Paul's greatest mystical sayings.
'I no longer' = 'ouketi egoo' His complete identification with Christ has merged his personality with His Saviour.
'gave Himself' = 'paradontes' = 'gave Himself up, surrendered'.
'for me' = 'huper emoi' Chrysostom says: 'He appropriates to himself the love which belongs equally with the whole world.'

2v21 'for nothing' = 'doorean' adverbial accusative of ' doorea' = 'a gift', ie 'gratuitously'.

NOTES ON CHAPTER THREE.

3v1 'Who has bewitched you?' = 'tis humas ebaskanen...' First aorist active of 'baskainoo', an old word akin to 'faskoo' 'baskoo' = to speak, then to bring evil upon someone by the evil eye (hoodoo), to lead astray by evil arts. Here only in NT Papyri give several examples of the adjective 'abaskanta', the adverb 'abaskantoos' (unharmed by the evil eye), and the substantive 'baskania' = 'witchcraft'.

Lightfoot quotes a third century AD scientist, Alexander Aphrodisiensis, describing the eyes of witches: 'They discharge from their pupils, as it were, a poisonous and destructive ray, and this, entering through the eyes of the person to whom they bear malice, will overthrow his soul and nature.'

'clearly portrayed' = 'proegraphee' 2nd aorist passive indicative of 'prographoo' = 'to write beforehand, to set forth by public proclamation, to placard, post up'. Several papyri statements by fathers they would no longer be responsible for their son's debt. 'graphoo' sometimes used in the sense of painting.

'crucified' = 'estauroomenos' = perfect passive participle. 1Corinthians 2v2. Continuing effects in the present.

3v3 Double set of contrasts between beginning (enarxamenoi) and 'attain your goal' (epiteleisthe), and between 'with the Spirit' (pneumati) and 'by human effort' (sarki). Keen irony here.

'begin' and 'attain your goal'. Paul uses the identical words in Philippians 1v6, and very similar words in 2 Corinthians 8v6. The pair used in connection with the order of the rites at religious ceremonies.

3v4 'have you suffered' (better 'did you suffer?') = 'epathete' 2nd aorist indicative of 'paschoo'. Record of persecution in South Galatia, not North.

3v5 'does (He) give' = 'epichoreegoon' present active participle. See 2 Corinthians 9v10, 1 Peter 1v5. = to furnish a chorus at one's own expense (eg for a civic festival), then 'to supply' in general.

'miracles' = 'dunameis' from verb 'dunamai' = 'I can, I am able', the power to perform something extraordinary, not necessarily miraculous (connections with 'dynamite' notwithstanding!). Two other words used for miracles are 'seemeia' = 'acts of significance, signs' and 'terata' = 'acts of wonder, awe-inspiring acts'.

3v6 See Romans 4v3ff to prove Abraham's faith was reckoned 'for'='with a view to ('eis'). James 2v23 uses a different episode in Abraham's life.

The original text is Genesis 15v6.

3v8 '(it) foresaw' = 'proidousa' 2 aorist active participle of 'prooraoo'. The Scripture is here personified.

The verse combines Genesis 12v3 and 18v18 in the Septuagint (Greek Old Testament), which use 'tribes' = 'phulai', and 'nations' = 'ethnee' respectively.

3v10 'under a curse' = 'upo kataran' 'kata'= 'down', + 'ara' = 'imprecation'. Hanging over them like the sword of Damocles. See Romans 3 v9. The curse becomes effective when the law is violated.

3v11 'before God' = 'para tou Theoo' = 'by the side of", ie from His perspective.

3v13 'He redeemed us' = 'heemas exeegorasen' 1st aorist active of 'exagorazoo' = 'to buy from, by back, ransom'. Slave purchase.

'the curse' = 'tees kataras'. Christ became a curse 'over' ('huper') us, and so came between us and the overhanging curse which fell on Him instead of us.

'a tree' = 'xulou' '(piece of)wood' rather than tree'. Allusion was to dead bodies on stakes or crosses. Joshua 10v26.

3v14 'that we might receive' = 'hina laboomen'. Hina introduces a clause of purpose, co-ordinate with the first clause here, 'in order that the **blessing...'**

3v15 'established' = 'kekuroomeneen' perfect passive participle, 'authoritative confirmation' from 'kuroo' = 'to ratify, make valid.

3v16. The promise to Abraham uses 'sperma' = 'seed' as a collective noun applying to each believer, used here as singular noun by Paul, adapting Rabbinic-style argument with Messianic significance.

3v17. '430 years' – 'tetrakosia kai triakonto etee' The Septuagint in Exodus 12 v40 adds words to include time of patriarchs in Canaan, which would halve their time in Egypt.

3v19 'because of ' = 'charin' adverbial accusative (direct object case) of 'charis', used as a preposition with the genitive (possessive case). It has telic force, (ie achieves a telos = goal or target) 'to make transgressions palpable'

3v20 No middlemen between God and Abraham - a difficult verse.

3v22 'a prisoner' = 'sunekleisen' 1st aorist active indicative of 'sungkleioo' = 'to shut together on all sides', like a shoal of fish trapped in a net.

Hume points out that enclosing and fencing in is as much a protective act as it is an imprisonment.

3v24 'put in charge' = 'paidagoogos'. Better-class families employed a slave in charge of a child from age 6-16. the pedagogue is now dismissed. We are in the school: of the Master... so no longer need a 'Minder'.

3v26 'sons' = 'huioi'. The usual word for children is 'tekna', which gives a sense of immaturity.

3v27 '(you) have clothed yourselves' = 'enedusasthe' 1st aorist middle of 'enduoo', as a badge or uniform of service.

3v29 Progressive and sequential argument. See Romans 8 v 29.

NOTES ON CHAPTER FOUR.

4v1 ' a child' = 'neepios' Under age.
Literally 'an infant', Vulgate 'parvalus', a minor of unspecified age.

4v2 'guardians' = 'epitropous', = 'trustees', and 'stewards' = 'oikonomous' = 'managers'.

4v3 'principles' = 'stoicheia', from 'stoichos' = 'a layer, or row', like letters of the alphabet. Or figures in a column. Hence 'the elements, principles, ordered sequence'. Development of angelic hierarchy in the inter-Testamental period, and the sequence of emanations, the 'ladder to God' of Gnosticism. See Colossians 2v8,15. Here, the conventional laws of the kosmos, or even of Jewish law, which exerted pressure or bondage of a kind.
'we were in slavery' = 'eemetha dedouloomenoi' the roundabout usage and perfect participle suggest a continuing condition.

4v4 Paul stresses the Jewishness of Jesus because being a Jew made Jesus subject to the law.
'the time had fully come' = 'to pleerooma tou chronou' Some say 'pleeroma' = 'that which fills' (active sense), but passive sense 'that which has been completed, filled' is better. Not the last drop, but the brimful container... 'chronos' time is a longer duration of (clock) time, 'chairos' is a limited moment of (opportune) time.

4v6 "our' = 'heemoon'. Paul switches pronouns 'your' to 'our' to be inclusive. No need to accept alternative text.
4v8 -9 Their bondage was understandable if they did not know God. But now ('nun de') they should be rejoicing in freedom, so if they are not, that is not understandable, because they now know God. Note the variant use of the words 'eidotes' in verse 8 and 'gnontes' in verse 9, indicating a change in relationship through God's grace.
'know' = 'eidotes', from 'oida' = more general word for knowing.
'known' = 'gnontes', from 'ginooskoo', which is usually knowledge

of a person. Here the initiative in knowing is with God.
'weak and miserable principles' = ' ta asthenee kai ptoocha stoicheia' It is probably better to understand this in relation to the pagan rather than the Jewish calendar.
'and...and...and' = 'kai...kai...kai' ironical reference to the rigmarole of this observance.

4v11 'I fear for you' = 'phoboumai humas'. He expresses fears in respect of their future, if they continue on their present course.

4v12 'You have done me no wrong' = 'ouden me eedikeesate' may be understating the case (litotes). 'I cannot say that I had reason to complain of you.'

4v13 'because of an illness' = 'di' astheneian' either with 'dia' used with an accompanying circumstance, or causally where his illness becomes the cause of his preaching the gospel. 'astheneia' could be a general state of eg exhaustion rather than a specific illness, eg eye disease, malaria, epilepsy.
'you did not treat me with contempt or scorn' = 'ouk exoutheneesate oude exeptusate' His illness was a visual trial to them, and they were perhaps tempted to despise or disregard him.

4v17 'to alienate'= 'ekkleisai' the idea is to shut out the Galatians, and cut them off from other influences. Egotistical zeal...

4v18 'it is a fine thing to be zealous' = 'kalon de zeelousthai'. Zeal is a fine thing, if it has a good object.

4v19 ' the pains of childbirth' = 'oodinoo' an intimate picture. See 1 Thessalonians 1v7.
4v21-2 'are you not aware?' = 'ouk akouete', literally 'don't you hear?', personifying Scripture as the 'speaker'.
Tender, but lively and penetrating tone (hoi hupo) nomon = 'the law' No article in Greek text – stresses the quality and standard of law.

4v23 'the slave-girl' = 'paidiskee'   a young girl, and here, a slave girl.

4v24   'they may be taken figuratively' = 'hatina estin alleegoroumena'
Can mean either : 'to speak in allegory' as here, or 'to expound in allegory'.
(dictionary definition of allegory = story, play, picture, poem in which the message is given symbolically)

4v25   Hagar...Sinai = 'Hagar...Sina'.   Hard to link the two. Unlikely that it is linguistic, from Arabic 'Hadjar' = stone, in Sinai area. Probably better to link with Jerusalem, like Sinai, a place of bondage (to law).

NOTES ON CHAPTER FIVE.

5v1 'For freedom' = 'tee eleutheria' The dative here is sometimes understood as instrumental.   Better, a dative of purpose . Ridderbos: 'Very emphatically the freedom of believers is placed in the foreground here as the purpose of Christ's redemptive work.'
'do (not) be burdened' = 'enechesthe'.   Present tense points to a new, continuous condition were they to listen to the false teachers.
'enechomai' is a legal term, = 'to be bound by' or 'to be liable to'.

5v3   'I declare' = 'marturomai', used when making a solemn statement before witnesses, and in a pagan context, before the gods.
'Again' = 'palin'   Paul is now repeating in relation to law what he had said in verse 2 in relation to Christ.

5v4 'you..have been alienated' = 'kateergeetheete'. 'katargoumai apo' = 'to be cut off from relations with someone, to have nothing further to do with something.'
'you have fallen away' = 'exepesate'. Originally used for the falling out of a flower. To be loosed from something, lose one's grasp of...

5v6 'in Christ' = 'en... Christoo' dative of sphere, the parameters of operation for the salvation granted through Him.
'expressing itself through love' = 'di' agapees energoumenee'
'energoumenee' is definitely middle, and answers the Roman Catholic exegesis which makes love rather than faith the normative idea. Faith reveals and verifies itself through love.

5v7 "who cut in' = 'tis ... enekopsen' literally 'knocked in' or 'barged in', a military term for demolition of bridges.

5v10 'I am confident' = 'egoo pepoitha' The 'egoo' gives a strongly personal quality ot this statement – 'I cannot for the life of me think otherwise..'

5v11 Paul is using himself as a hypothetical case. He was not promoting circumcision.
'the offence' = 'skandalon'. Originally the bit of stick which keeps the trap from falling until one touches it. Hence, the occasion for sinning or falling, ie a stumbling-block.

5v12 'emasculate' = 'apokopsontai' The word is used with this meaning in the profane authors. Self-mutilation was practised in the cult of Attis, whose most famous temples were in Rome, and in Phrygia in Asia Minor.
The verb 'apokoptoo' is used of cutting off hands or feet in Mark 9v43, 45 and of cutting off ears in John 18v10,26.

5v13 'to indulge' = 'aphormee', a compound word, 'apo' + 'hormaoo' = 'point of departure, bridgehead, launching-pad' See Romans 7v11.

5v14 'the entire law' = 'ho pas nomos' is the law considered as an integrated unit, as distinguished from the individual commandments.

'is summed up' = 'pepleerootai' The verb has the force, not only of the doing of the law, but includes its interpretation. The perfect tense combines the sense of the definitive with the continuing.

5v15 'you will be destroyed' = 'avalootheete'. Aorist subjunctive. Unfulfilled condition – things have not yet reached this low ebb.

5v16 'you will not' = 'ou mee' When this is taken with the aorist subjunctive or aorist indicative, it is the most decisive form of denying a future event.

5v17 'so that' = 'hina mee' – the 'hina' may be taken as either final or consecutive, latter preferred, because it would join opposing principles (flesh and spirit) as the subject.

5v20 'witchcraft' = 'pharmakeia' covers a wide range of activities involving drugs, spells and magic potions.

'fits of rage' = 'thumoi' originally, 'breath' then disposition. In NT = an outburst or eruption of passion or wrath.

'factions' = 'haireseis' comes from 'haireomai' = to choose. Then to choose between opinions, then 'divisions'.

5v25 'let us keep in step' = 'stoichoomen' from 'stoichoo'. It is more rigid than the 'peripatein' of verse 16. The idea of a row or rule is contained in it. It is used for movement in a definite line, as in a military formation, or in dancing.

5v26. 'conceited' = 'kenodoxoi' A person becomes like this when he swaggers or brags, which is provoking and challenging. The person who wants to be first cannot stand the success of another.

NOTES ON CHAPTER SIX.

6v1 'caught' = 'proleemphthee' Meaning uncertain. Some say = 'to be overcome, taken unawares, by sin. The other, and more likely possibility is that he is overtaken, from the following 'in a sin' = 'en tini paraptooma', conveying the idea of mistake rather than misdeed. Unwitting rather than deliberate or planned sin, but nevertheless a responsible act of sin.

6v2 'burdens' = 'baree' = oppressive load, which bows us down and makes us fear we will buckle under its pressure. Different from the fitting load pictured in verse 5 ('phortion'). The Galatian Christians must give mutual support, while carrying personal loads appropriate to their capacities.

6v4 'test' = 'dokimazetoo'. 'dokimazoo' means to approve after testing, as each one weighs and assesses his own work.

6v5 The guilt of another person does not excuse me.

6v6 'in all good things' = 'en pasin agathois' = pupils have a responsibility to give material and financial support to their teachers.
See Romans 15v27 and 1 Corinthians 9v4-14.

6v9 'let us not become weary' = 'mee engkakoomen' See also Luke 18v1 for use in this sense.
'good' = 'kalos' really means 'the beautiful, the lovely', visually as well as ethically.
'we do not give up' = ' mee ekluomenoi', like unstringing a bow, or going out of physical condition.

6v10 'good' = this time the form is 'agathon' instead of the 'kalon' of verse 9. The good in a comprehensive sense, specifically expressed in a favourable attitude towards others. (see 5v22)

6v11 'letters' = 'grammasin' can mean 'letter, epistle'. Generally accepted that 'letters' is the right version. Paul uses 'epistolee' for 'letter'.

6v14 'boast' = 'kauchaomai', not always in a bad sense, see verse 4. Paul uses the verb at least 34 times in his letters.

6v17 'the marks' = 'ta stigmata' = tattoos?   Brand for protection?
Point is fellowship with Christ, not cultic property rights.
'I bear' = 'bastazoo' rather than 'echoo' = 'I have', so that Paul will display the stigmata like trophies of war or sport.